PRACTIC

THE WEISER CONCISE GUIDE SERIES

PRACTICAL ASTROLOGY

PRISCILLA COSTELLO, M.A.

EDITED AND INTRODUCED BY
JAMES WASSERMAN

WEISERBOOKS
San Francisco, CA / Newburyport, MA

First published in 2008 by
Red Wheel/Weiser, LLC
With offices at:
500 Third Street, Suite 230
San Francisco, CA 94107
www.redwheelweiser.com

ISBN: 978-1-57863-423-1
Library of Congress Cataloging-in-Publication Data
available upon request

Cover design by Maija Tollefson
Book design and production by Studio 31
www.studio31.com

Typeset in Adobe Sabon
Cover illustration © Camille Flammarion/Corbis Images

Printed in Canada
TCP
10 9 8 7 6 5 4 3 2 1

TABLE OF CONTENTS

ACKNOWLEDGMENTS

THIS BOOK IS A DISTILLATION of over thirty years of study. I am indebted to the many authors and teachers I have encountered along the way. One of the most important was Richard Idemon, a San Francisco-based astrologer from whom I learned the method of weighting chart factors decribed in Part II.

Attending innumerable workshops and conferences over the years, both as participant and speaker, as well as serving on the boards of astrological organizations in both the United States and Canada, has allowed me to meet many well-known thinkers and practitioners in the field. In particular, lectures and workshops with Robert Hand, one of the founders of Project Hindsight (formed to translate ancient texts on astrology from Greek and Latin into modern English) have always been brilliant and inspiring. I have been fortunate to study astrology with the best minds in the field, including Alan Oken, Liz Greene, Stephen Arroyo, and John Addey and Charles Harvey of the British Astrological Association.

My deepest thanks to Donald Weiser and Yvonne Paglia, who introduced me to Jim Wasserman, the project editor for this series. Jim offered me the opportunity to write this book, and has been a courageous advocate for it, as well as a consistently helpful guide through the publishing process.

Many people, besides those mentioned above, have taught, inspired, and shared ideas with me, and have assisted with shaping the various drafts. Paul Craig (a non-astrologer) read and annotated it in detail, offering a multitude of intelligent and insightful observations. Wendy Guy (an excellent astrologer herself) did a thorough Virgoan read of the text and made many specific and astute suggestions for its improvement. Members of the Astrology Book Club in Toronto (Mary Wiens, Michael Barwick, and Barbara Rodrigoe) read and commented on some sections. I am indebted to Michael Barwick, Wendy Guy, and Ursula Fugger, who added to the list of web sites, and to Janet Markham (head of the Canadian Association for Astrological Education) and Wendy Guy, who contributed to the recommended reading list.

Introduction

by

James Wasserman

The strongest compliment I can pay to Priscilla Costello is to reveal that I allowed her to do my chart. Now that may not sound as important to the reader as it is to me, so a word of explanation. I had my first experience with tarot and astrology in 1967. I learned that the state of mind attendant upon seeking universal truth in a reading from another person required a level of openness I needed to be cautious about extending promiscuously.

I have since had several experiences of either incorrect data or astrologers seeking to advance an agenda. Once, I lost a great deal of money after being told my business would double. It actually did, but in the wrong direction! I lost my biggest client at the moment of predicted expansion. When I sought a follow-up strategy discussion with the astrologer, I found myself in contact with an answering machine.

On the other hand, I have experienced unbelievable accuracy from astrologers. That's almost part of the problem. Between their skill and our willingness to believe lies a perilous minefield for a spiritually aware person who seeks to protect his or her magical integrity from misinformation, while seeking guidance from extra-personal sources.

Upon meeting Priscilla, I was delighted to find a sane, intelligent, perceptive, warm, canny, mature, spiritual woman with a sense of humor. She also had perhaps that most important of qualities—the ability not to take herself too seriously. She was also an absolute encyclopedia of astrological information, the equal of only three other astrologers I've known. I needed help with a decision, so after several agonizing months, I finally popped the question. And I haven't needed to look back ever since.

In fact, after that first reading, I asked her to write this book. And now it's your turn to say hello to a brilliant and insightful woman whose carefully crafted and structured approach to astrology is unlike any you'll find. This book truly provides the key to hidden treasure.

Priscilla's data on the components of astrology—signs, planets, etc.—is exhaustive, as might be expected. However, what is striking is how elevated, sophisticated, and interesting her insights into these fundamentals are. She leads the reader step-by-step through an in-depth demonstration of the practical use of the information in chart interpretation. No matter how experienced or familiar you are with astrology, you will learn more than you expect. And I can think of no better introduction for a beginner.

Everything you need to begin or expand your knowledge of astrology is contained right here, including a comprehensive list of the best resources to continue your study.

I especially enjoy Priscilla's optimism. The pessimistic, determinative, depressive school of astrology leaves me cold. Priscilla teaches us how to make lemonade from lemons, details the transformative lessons of difficult astrological placements, and embodies a "can do" attitude throughout her interpretation.

If you study this book with diligence, you will be able to read an astrological chart—your own or that of another—with some competence. You will learn to focus a lens of perception on the interaction of heaven and earth, and appreciate the miracle of the unity of the divine incarnate within the multiplicity of the human. You will gain a penetrating insight into some of the cosmic energies that compose and sustain our eternally resonant Universe.

A Brief Overview

Astrology is a rich and complex language of symbols that encompasses all aspects of human experience. Learning to speak this language enables you to think in new and creative ways about yourself and the world.

This book introduces you to the basic principles of astrology—the grammar of its nouns, adjectives, and verbs, if you like—from the perspective of the philosophical and esoteric world view of which astrology is a part. After reading it, you will understand where its grammar originated and how it relates to other esoteric studies, as well as have some practical skills to analyze horoscopes—your own and others'. It will also help you to see the richness and depth of astrological interpretation—a surprise to those who are familiar with only the Sun-sign predictions found in magazines, newspapers, and online.

PART I elucidates the four essential categories: eight PLANETS plus the Sun and Moon; the twelve zodiacal SIGNS, each representing typical roles or approaches to life; the twelve HOUSES, each marking significant areas of life experience; and the ASPECTS, the geometrical relationships between planets that reveal the degree of concord or discord between the celestial bodies.

Volumes could be—and have been—written on each of these components of astrology. To make this indeed a "concise guide," I have concentrated on these essentials and deliberately omitted many other factors, such as the Moon's nodes, asteroids, "Arabic" parts, fixed stars, newly identified planets, and points. You can explore these later as you expand your study. In the beginning, it is best to be grounded in the basics that establish a firm foundation for astrological mastery.

PART II provides a method for synthesizing and evaluating the four primary elements (planets, signs, houses, and aspects) so you can grasp the whole and interpret the symbolic picture yourself.

An elementary knowledge of these basics can be immensely useful and emotionally affirming. With such knowledge, you can penetrate your inner psychology more deeply and see the panorama of your unfolding life cycles. Meditating on your chart gives you an opportunity for self-reflection and life evaluation, and can confirm an intuitive sense of your life's purposes and patterns. Since your chart's meaning unfolds gradually over time, as you engage deeper levels, it becomes an inexhaustible source of insights. And, if you are interested in such pursuits, sustained focus on the symbols of astrology increases the contemplative ability of your mind to penetrate beyond the literal.

You can also understand others more compassionately and discover the dynamics of your relationships with them: partner to partner, parent to child, employee to boss. Looking at charts of countries and companies or grasping the rhythms of repeating planetary cycles through the centuries gives insight into sweeping political, economic, cultural, and historical trends. Astrology is an extraordinarily practical study.

Once learned, these basics can be applied to whatever area most interests you: the course of an illness, the direction of the stock market, or the fate of nations. You encounter them again and again, like the shifting stones in a kaleidoscope, in charts of famous people, in charts of dramatic world events (like political elections or natural disasters), and in individual predictive work. Because the same factors are always present—sometimes in the background, sometimes in the foreground—it is fruitful to return periodically to these four key categories of planets, signs, houses, and aspects.

Astrology is also classified as an esoteric study. Esoteric disciplines use an encoded symbolic language to convey hidden truths. For practicing ceremonial magicians, alchemists, or Kabbalists, a knowledge of astrology is indispensible—if only for the timing of experiments, meditative practices, or public or private rituals. Pagans, especially Wiccans, time their gatherings at Full Moons, and sometimes New Moons too.

How then can astrology, with such wide-ranging uses, be defined? **Astrology is the calculation and meaningful interpretation of the positions and motions of the heavenly bodies, and their correlation with human experience.** The main tool of delineation, the horoscope, is a snapshot of the planetary positions in the zodiac at the moment of birth, constructed by using the longitude and latitude of the birthplace and the time of birth.

Astrology's central concept is succinctly stated as "interconnectedness" or "correspondence." In the ancient world view from which astrology emerged, the universe unfolds from the invisible into the visible dimensions in a great linked chain. It proceeds from the Godhead down through the realms of the fixed stars and planets, which some equate with ten levels of archangels and angels. It continues to the mundane world, which derives its character and identity from mixtures of the four elements: fire, air, water, and earth. (These are not literally the elements you can see and touch, but more abstract principles.)

The entire Universe is a single conscious and intelligent entity, with each of the unfolding parts corresponding in design to levels above, and in sympathetic resonance with like elements on all levels. Since human beings reflect the cosmic order, every aspect of our physical and psychic structure displays similarities to the cosmos. Another way of saying this is that the microcosm (the familiar world in which we live) is intimately linked to the macrocosm (the greater cosmos). Literally, our earthly experience is reflected in the heavenly realm.

This ancient perspective is found in the second statement of the Emerald Tablet, a document ascribed to Hermes Trismegistus (or "thrice-great"), a teacher, ruler, and sage in ancient Egypt who inaugurated the Western esoteric tradition. It can be translated as follows: "What is below is like what is above, and what is above is like what is below, to accomplish the wonders of the one thing."* In our modern, more psychologically oriented, time, "as within, so without" expresses a similar idea.

Astrology has been an integral part of every major civilization on our planet, both Eastern and Western: Babylonian/Sumerian, Egyptian, Greek, Roman, Chinese, Indian, and Meso-American. It has flourished in times of heightened intellectual and creative ferment, like the Renaissance. It is a nearly universal language describing the interaction between humanity and the cosmos, its language crossing cultures and enduring over time.

Recently, we have begun to understand that a butterfly can flap its wings in the Amazon and be connected to a snowfall in the Rockies. It is only one more step to see synchronicity—that is, meaningful coincidences—between the movements of planets and other bodies with events on Earth. Such a viewpoint opens us to the philosophical and spiritual dimensions of astrology.

Our culture can benefit immensely from rediscovering this means of perception. The scientific (mechanistic/materialistic)

---

* Richard Smoley, trans. *Gnosis* magazine, Summer 1996, p. 18.

paradigm that emerged in the 18th century focused its attention relentlessly on the physical world, and ignored—even denied—the existence of God, soul, or consciousness. It left the modern individual alienated from nature, inhabiting a meaningless universe, and often living a compartmentalized existence— acknowledging divinity one day a week, but being materially oriented the other six. Any study that reveals our profound connection to the whole and enables us to see recurrent and connected patterns in our lives can restore psychic balance and wholeness. Our culture, our environment, our planet, all desperately need that.

As you discover astrology's depth and complexity, you may feel overwhelmed by the amount of information to be digested and retained. If you experience this, take breaks between sessions of study and contemplation. Students commonly feel inundated by all the information because, unlike other symbolic languages like physics or mathematics, astrology deals with archetypes. That is, astrological language references a dimension with a reality above and beyond the visible one—a realm of ideas in the Platonic sense that manifests itself in multiple ways. Besides memorizing long lists of associations, it is helpful to ponder these symbols over time, meditating on them to allow all their meanings to emerge.

Along with its practical, philosophical, and spiritual dimensions, astrology has an almost mystical aspect. Engaging it can lead to an illuminative experience that profoundly alters your attitudes and beliefs. Uncovering the extraordinary way in which your character and life are both an emanation of and an interaction with higher energies can be mind-stunning—another reason I recommend you absorb it slowly.

Astrology connects us to many other studies: Babylonian and Egyptian religion and astronomy, Greek mathematics and philosophy, esoteric and spiritual studies like alchemy, numerology, or Kabbalah, as well as contemporary psychology (especially Carl Jung's). In the chapters that follow, I will allude to these to clarify astrology's history and tradition and to explore other aspects of how and where astrological ideas and techniques originated.

Part One:

The Theory of Astrology

CHAPTER ONE

THE PLANETS: THE FIRST PIECE

ASTROLOGY CONSISTS OF GROUPS OF SYMBOLS, all having numerological and philosophical, as well as psychological and literal, meanings. The seven classical planets, plus the three more recently discovered Uranus, Neptune, and Pluto, are the main letters of the astrological alphabet. (The word "planets" is used throughout to apply to the Sun and Moon, though technically the Sun is a minor star and the Moon a satellite of Earth. To indicate that the Sun and Moon are considered as astrological archetypes, they are capitalized.) Planets are the factors that transmit energy in steps from the Godhead into the created world. Each is named for a Roman god or goddess whose character and history is largely borrowed from the Greek mythological tradition.

In psychological terms, the planets are carriers of psychic energy, responsible for the uniqueness and dynamism of each individual. They are motivators, impelling you to seek experiences and passively attracting them. In psychological language, they are equivalent to "needs" or "drives."

The number seven may be considered sacred precisely because there were originally believed to be seven planets (including Sun and Moon). The seven-day week was created with each day corresponding to one of them. A host of other associations also arose— metals, colors, rocks and precious gems, perfumes and incense, herbs, trees and plants, animals, emblems, and deities of various cultures. Whatever idea was associated with a planet was thought to have an affinity with its nature, on its own particular level. Astrological correlations derive in part from specific observations of physical reality. Because physical reality reflects inner essence, shape, appearance, taste, and behavior, all reveal planetary connections. Birthstones linked to the months of the year are a simplified example of astrological correspondence.

Given the archetypal nature of astrological symbols, the traditional way to learn about them is to memorize and ponder lists of key words. But you cannot grasp their significance with the intellect alone. You must *circle* the symbols, musing on a cluster of associated concepts to penetrate their essence. This is the method I use in the sections that follow: a circumambulation of each symbol that explores the concepts associated with it. At some point, with study and reflection on a given symbol, you may have an "aha!" moment of insight when you intuitively comprehend its inner meaning.

We will study the planets' basic principles and explore some literal manifestations, psychological meanings, and connections to various esoteric, religious, or spiritual disciplines. The discussion moves freely, referring to the essential planetary principle, the god or goddess that embodies it, or the many possible associated externalizations in our time-space dimension.

It is sometimes difficult in talking about astrology to find language that does not sound causal. Even though the planets represent pure abstract essences, astrologers as a shorthand always end up saying "it" or "he" or "she" "does" that or "influences" this or "rules" such-and-such. You must understand, however, that the planets are not *causing* anything—that astrology works because there is a greater organizing principle behind the appearance—synchronicity, that *includes both the planets and us*. We talk as if it were causal for convenience. But the planets (or any other factor) don't make you *do* anything, any more than the clock makes you put down your work at 5:00 and go home, or turn on the TV at 8:00 to see your favorite show.

The following ideas are intended to be suggestive and not definitive; you will benefit from reading other astrology books, consulting symbol dictionaries, and researching esoteric references to further open each symbol's inner meaning. Because a symbol's expression may be multivarious and not entirely predictable, one fascinating aspect of learning the astrological language is to observe how the universe plays with possibilities in manifesting planetary potential.

Some planets, like the Sun and Moon, or Venus and Mars, are obvious complementary opposites. According to some esoteric theories, at the moment of creation, the invisible One broke into a visible two, appearing as opposites that characterize our world: light and dark, up and down, good and bad, masculine and feminine, and so on. Some planetary pairs perfectly represent these polarized extremes.

Each astrological symbol also reflects this duality by containing *within itself* both an up side and a down side. In the old days (before the 20th century!), some of the symbols (like Saturn) were thought to be exclusively negative, and others (like Jupiter) exclusively positive. This interpretive bias has changed in the modern period, as greater psychological sophistication and awareness of esoteric ideas has led to the realization that symbols inherently contain their opposites.

The "Lights": The Sun and the Moon

THE SUN (☉)

The Sun has received most attention in popular culture, because people know their birthdate (which immediately reveals the Sun's position in the zodiac). It can thus be isolated and commercially exploited. However, the Sun truly is the essential symbol. In fact, "essence" or "essential nature" are solar keywords.

The Sun is the paramount symbol of life, since its energy makes all living things active. The east, where the Sun rises with increasing splendor, is the place of birth or the first emergence of life. The Sun's reappearance each morning means that dark night is vanquished once more and that life will continue. The very predictability of sunrise each day lends human life order and stability.

Like the Sun, the solar hero or savior delivers his people from dark and monstrous terrors—even death itself. One such semi-divine hero is the Greek Perseus, whose mother conceived him in a shower of gold, the metal of the Sun. Perseus freed his people from tyrannical rule and destroyed the snake-haired Medusa, whose glance literally petrified anyone who gazed upon her. In myth, solar heroes like Perseus break free from the influence of parents and culture and overcome inner fears to reveal the individual's most glorious possibilities. These heroes, like the Sun itself, embody the elemental masculine principle.

But too much solar energy is destructive; it burns, dries, and dessicates, destroying crops and threatening life. The Chinese shot arrows at the Sun to challenge its deadly rays, which can magically transform invisible heat into visible fire.

Because of the Sun's prominence in the sky and the power of its rays, it represents divinity—the all-seeing eye of Ra in Egypt or Odin's eye of wisdom in Norse tradition. Under its steady gaze, all things are fully illumined and starkly differentiated. But the Sun's warm rays also translate as love from the divine heart, poured out freely to all on Earth.

By analogy, the Sun represents not only God in the heavens, but a nation's king on Earth. The ruler in many cultures was the "son of the Sun"; such a title presumed that he would rule with the same power as his heavenly counterpart. Since the Sun's rays fall with equal warmth on all, the ruler was expected to be just and impartial.

Being the outstanding symbol of illumination, the Sun is also the light of reason within the individual, enabling the declaration "I see!" at a moment of dawning insight. Reason is more than intellect. Sun gods like Apollo were often gifted with prophecy. The Sun is spiritual illumination, depicted as halos around the heads of saints or golden auras around enlightened beings.

The most intriguing and contradictory interpretation of the Sun has to do with the concept of the self. Psychologically, the Sun is the ego, the center of personal consciousness. But this personal self is a constructed or false (that is, temporary) self that is useful only in this world.

Yet the Sun also symbolizes the greater Self, the divine spark within, the inner core of the individual, all-encompassing and immortal, residing in the heart yet filling the entire cosmos. In spiritual terms, focusing on the Sun rather than on Earth means basing your sense of self not on ego but on eternal spirit. The individual who makes this shift of identification is "twice-born," and may experience the mystic vision whose splendor is like the rising of a thousand Suns.

Thus the Sun is paradoxically both the "lower" and the "higher" self: the personality that is an essential actor in this world, and the true Self that is your real identity. Our task seems to be to walk a kind of razor's edge: to be simultaneously the personal expression of the Sun and the impersonal bearer of the inner light.

THE MOON (☽)

Unlike the Sun, the Moon is continually waxing and waning—first invisible at the dark New Moon, then an emerging crescent, next a fully visible orb, and finally back to crescent and invisibility again. So it symbolizes impermanence and constant change. No wonder Juliet urges Romeo, "O swear not by the Moon, the inconstant Moon ... "

In moonlight, things lose color. Separate things merge into one. Another kind of seeing, a diffused whole-body perception, overshadows rationality. Thus the Moon represents instinctual knowing without the use of logic. In esotericism, moonlight is analogous to the "astral light" of an invisible plane above the material where the principal organ of perception is the imagination. Things and ideas can come into being instantaneously and magically as the creative imagination conceives them.

The Moon symbolizes fertility, the Great Mother who gives birth to new forms of life and oversees their subsequent growth within vegetable, animal, and human kingdoms. Fertility is often measured in lunar cycles: farmers and gardeners plant, prune, and harvest according to the Moon's phases; a human female's fertility correlates to the changing Moon. Modern research has shown that at the Full Moon both animal and human sexual activity increases. Altogether, the Moon represents the entire process of the coming into being and the passing away of forms.

The Moon measures time. The earliest calendars were based on lunar cycles, marked by notches in bone that tracked New and Full Moons and eclipses. Days and years were established by the rising and setting Sun in its seasons, but intermediate periods were set by the Moon, whose rounds established the week and month ("moonth"). Lunar calendars are still used by some religions (Judaism and Islam) and cultures. The Chinese New Year is always the first New Moon in Aquarius; Easter's date is fixed as the first Sunday following the first New Moon after the Spring Equinox.

As keeper of time, the Moon means mortality. All visible life is subject to change, as forms materialize, fluctuate in their appearance, and then disappear—just like the Moon which dwindles and "dies" each month during its dark phase. It therefore measures human fate. Moon goddesses are often portrayed as spinners or weavers of destiny, like the Norse three Norns, or the three Fates of ancient Greece who spun, measured, and cut the threads of life on the loom of time.

The Moon relates to water in all its forms: the water of the womb, the water that falls as rain or appears magically as morning dew, and the vast ocean whose rising and ebbing tides are attributed to the Moon's attractive pull.

The Moon is the preeminent symbol of the feminine principle. It is associated with emotions, the inward, fluid tides of feeling that fluctuate from moment to moment, and instinctual urges and subliminal drives that motivate us without our personal will in control.

First differentiated in ancient Greece, the three principal phases of the Moon—new, full, and waning—correlate to three stages of a woman's life: maiden, mother, and crone (or wise woman). Differentiating the Moon allowed for contradictory interpretations such as virginal or maternal, barren or fertile, chaste or seductive. These aspects were represented by three distinct goddesses: Artemis the virgin huntress, Hera the wife, and Hecate the wise woman. No wonder, with her changeability and varied guises, that the feminine principle is seen as mysterious and unfathomable, irrational and unknowable.

Psychologically, the Moon represents the unconscious, the primitive and largely unknowable part of ourselves, the "night" half of the psyche. Remarkably, the Moon always has the same face toward Earth: its dark side is never seen.

The realm of the unconscious is notoriously difficult to engage without losing psychic balance; you must face fears and fantasies, and unmask projections. In esoteric terms, this has to do with the initiatory experience of confronting the "dweller on the threshold," a fear-inspiring entity that blocks your progress. This figure constellates everything you dread and have repressed, explaining why many find the inner explorations of therapy more terrifying than extreme sports.

In Kabbalistic mysticism, the Moon is the realm of Yesod, the first rung of the ladder of heaven, "the Treasurehouse of Images." Experiencing this dimension gives a vision of the workings of the Universe, and a perception of shapes before they coalesce and appear as physical forms.

The Five Classical Planets

MERCURY (☿)

The planet Mercury travels so close to the Sun that it can rarely be seen. No wonder the god Mercury is shown with a cap of invisibility! The planet moves the fastest of any, so the god Mercury wears a winged hat and has wings on his heels. Mercury correlates with the ability to move quickly and to adapt instantly to new situations, as well as to physical agility and manual dexterity—like that used by the juggler or stage magician who entertains to delight or fool the eye.

Because of Mercury's closeness to the Sun, it was natural to interpret its archetype as the gods' messenger. Thus Mercury is the mind, the rational faculty that clothes divine ideas in everyday words. Not only is it the power of the spoken word itself, but also your manner of thinking and speaking, the style and quality of your communication.

Mercury is the childlike curiosity that drives your urge to know and matures into the ability to reason and analyze the information gathered. At its most developed, Mercury is eloquence and persuasiveness. In ancient Greece, honey was sacrificed to him as the literal God of Sweet-talk. Mercury encompasses the sophisticated art of rhetoric, the glibness of a car salesman, the sly subversiveness of a town gossip, and the propaganda of a political machine.

In Latin, *mercari* means "to engage in business," and Mercury rules trade and commerce—the selling, bartering, and negotiating of the marketplace, and the merchant class that arises from it. The negative side of Mercury is a cleverness that succumbs to trickery and deceit—and at an extreme, to lying and outright thievery. Mercury is the Trickster, a god who plays games with human beings, sometimes for sheer sport and sometimes to shatter their self-generated illusions.

The first myth told about Mercury is that on the very day of his birth, he stole Apollo's cattle. Forced to return them by his father, Jupiter, he placated Apollo with a gift. He created the first lyre by taking a turtle's shell and stringing it with nine linen cords, in honor of the nine Muses. Apollo was so impressed with Mercury's inventiveness that he gave him the caduceus, a rod with two serpents entwined around it with wings on top. The caduceus has become the symbol of the healing profession. Esoterically, it may also represent the risen kundalini, the energetic fire of the body that surges up the spine through the dual channels of ida and pingala, and creates an energy field that heals all who sit within its range. The caduceus is the inner wand of the true magician, whose powers derive from an illumined consciousness.

Mercury not only bestows ordinary knowledge, but also whispers hidden truths. Part of the esoteric magician's special knowledge is the ritualistic use of language, a reflection of the creative Logos that literally brought the world into being through the spoken Word.

Mercury not only relayed messages from heaven to Earth, but also (as Hermes Psychopompus, his Greek name) conducted souls from Earth to the underworld. Because of his unique ability to cross boundaries, he became the patron of travel and the god of roads. Herms, or pillars, are often found at crossroads, especially where three ways intersect.

Mercury is often portrayed as androgynous. He is the still-somewhat-undifferentiated offspring of the Sun and the Moon with both male and female physical characteristics. As the alchemical hermaphrodite, he may also represent not just the unredeemed matter of the alchemist's early experiments but the final outcome of his efforts—the marriage of the Sun and Moon, the restoration of all dualities into one.

Venus (♀)

Venus is the differentiated daughter of the divine, exclusively feminine. The eternal SHE, Venus is the well-recognized goddess of love and beauty. No wonder that flowers spring up behind her when she graces the Earth. Her attractive charisma is so powerful that she can draw to herself any lover she chooses. She is the free and independent courtesan or geisha, the never-married one. This innate power is enhanced by the feminine arts of fashion and personal adornment.

Venus governs art in general, as well as aesthetics, the study of the beautiful. Beautiful objects awaken not only an emotional but a spiritual response that leads us to contemplate an archetypal world of the Beautiful and the Good.

Venus' sterling qualities include charm, diplomacy, and tact, giving her a sociability leading to peace and harmony within society. But she is better known for inspiring personal romantic attraction and stirring sexual desire. She wants us to enjoy the physical pleasures that lead to joy, even ecstasy.

But these positive, even transcendent, possibilities for Venus are counterbalanced by her negative side. Her penchant for luxury can lead to self-indulgence. In love, she can be vengeful, jealous, envious, and, of course, unfaithful. Her sensuality can exhaust itself in lasciviousness and sheer lust.

Venus' sensual side is reflected in the story of her birth. According to one version, after Cronus severed his father Uranus' genitals and threw them into the Aegean Sea, Venus emerged from the fertile waters onto the shores of Cyprus as the "foam-born" (Greek *aphros* means "foam," hence her Greek name, Aphrodite). Venus could renew her virginity by bathing in these same waters.

Venus leads us into relationships, both for personal enjoyment and for greater psychological wholeness. She is the intiatrix into love's mysteries. For men, Venus is one aspect of their inner feminine side or anima, the ideal woman conceived in their imaginations. Activation of Venus can invite an awakening to love, as reflected in the Greek myth of Pygmalion and Galatea. Pygmalion created a statue of the ideal woman, and his prayers to Venus brought the statue, emblematic of his own frozen capacity for genuine connection, to vibrant life.

So Venus has a dual focus in loving. The sexual love she celebrates can be transformed into the experience of a sacred union, both with a lover and with the divinity behind the form. The temple prostitutes of ancient times may have been practicing a form of tantra, in which the goddess' devotees drew the participant into a holy communion of souls. Venus' domain of relationship can become a spiritual path leading to an open-heartedness to your partner and ultimately to the Self.

MARS (♂)

Exclusively male, Mars is the precise and complementary opposite of Venus in every way. Mars is the god of conflict, aggression, and outright war. Yet the traditional associations with Mars may be skewed too much to the negative (he was, in ancient times, called "the lesser malefic").

Mars was originally a god of agriculture for whom the month of March is named. He is dominant during spring, a time of the explosive energy of new life bursting forth from the Earth. He is connected with vitality, general energy level, and healthy self-assertion. He is the positive, active masculine expressed as conscious intention and the will power that transforms ideas into discernible achievements.

Mars is the heated passion behind action, both initiating and defensive. He is the heroism of defending one's home, country, and interests against others' attacks. In magical rituals, spikes made of iron (Mars' metal) were used to carve circles in the ground for protection against male demons.

This same fighting spirit is brought to the battlefield, where fearless courage brings victory. He loves to be physically active and, as a substitute for war, glories in the competitive world of sport, in which he uses his physically developed body and muscular strength to defeat rivals.

But whether on the field or in the arena, Mars' fiery energy easily slides into destructive fury. A red mist falls over the warrior's eyes and, possessed by the murderous rage of battle, he becomes an engine of death. No surprise, then, that Mars, dubbed "the red planet" because of its color, rules blood and bloodshed.

Mars also rules the sex drive, which, if corrupted, becomes rape, used as an instrument of war in the "battle of the sexes." The predatory male is a "wolf," the animal associated with Mars; the "lone wolf" is the alienated male, socially isolated and potentially disruptive of community. Certainly there is a primitive, untamed, and uncivilized quality to Mars. Its energy manifests as anger, impatience, frustration, irritation, and, at an extreme, cruelty and destructive violence. Only the loving and refining energy of Venus integrates Mars into self and society.

Psychologically, Mars manifests as the type of man a woman attracts, a projection of her inner male or animus. For a man, it is the image of the masculine, shaping the way he expresses his maleness.

On the Kabbalistic tree, Mars is linked to Geburah, the sphere of Power. As Robert Hand has pointed out, in this context it has a more collective than personal meaning: it is analogous to Shiva, the necessary energy of destruction that paves the way for new creation.

JUPITER (♃)

Jupiter is physically the largest of the planets, with an energy field that stretches throughout the solar system. As befits his size, mythologically he is the king of all the gods, first among the immortals, the supreme power. His authority was unquestioned. No wonder he signifies law and the justice that comes from a sovereign's sound judgment.

Jupiter is the Roman name for the last in a series of sky gods whose sphere was the blue vastness above the Earth. As lord of the heavens, he symbolizes the broad vista of the higher mind, which takes raw facts and information (Mercury), extracts their essential import, and organizes them into categories with long-term validity and wide application.

Psychologically, he is the search for truth or meaning. He governs philosophy, metaphysics, and religion, as well as education and the law. He is experience distilled into wisdom. His is the sure faith based on a belief in the essential beneficence of a moral Universe. He is the conviction that there is a just divinity who rewards the good and punishes the bad. He is the liberal outlook that believes in unending progress within an orderly world. He is light overcoming darkness, the power of right to vanquish lesser and lower forces.

Such an attitude leads to confidence and optimism, a positive mental outlook that attracts good fortune and prosperity. He is "good karma" that seems to come without much effort. As "the great benefactor," he generously bestows wealth, success, honors, gifts, and graces. Those blessed by Jupiter's abundance and liberality just seem lucky. No wonder he is jovial (Jove was the Romans' alternate name for Jupiter), friendly, and kindhearted—happy to be benevolent and to be appreciated for it. He is the all-wise father, the positive aspect of patriarchy. He oversees growth and expansion on every level. Politically, he correlates to a country's liberal party in its most exalted sense.

Jupiter is also protective spiritually. He is the guardian angel who preserves life and moderates fate. He operates as the Law of Grace that can mitigate punishment and override karmic law. He is mercy personified, the same mercy that, as Portia describes so perfectly in *The Merchant of Venice,* "... is not strained; it droppeth as the gentle rain of heaven."

By association with its symbol, the eagle that sees afar, Jupiter is connected with what is at a distance (foreign countries) and the long journeys taken to travel there. Jupiter's restless, adventurous spirit drives the wanderer or the seeker on a quest.

The ancients viewed Jupiter as unalloyedly positive (as the "greater benefic"), yet there are pitfalls in his expression. Though representing the law, he can begin to see himself as *above* the law:

haughty, arrogant, self-righteous. Restless and unsatisfied, nothing is ever enough or good enough. His drive to obtain more can lead to exaggeration and excess, over-indulgence bringing illness or ruin. He can be gross like the glutton, wasteful and extravagant like the gambler and spendthrift. He literally bites off more than he can chew. Viewing himself as the fecund male, literally "god's gift" to women, he can be the playboy or unfaithful husband.

But even overdoing can be educative, for over-indulgence can create feelings of disgust and a resulting detachment from desire. As William Blake said, "The road of excess leads to the palace of wisdom."

SATURN (♄)

Saturn, unlike Jupiter, is an energy of concentration, constriction, and constraint, all of which may annoy the ego but benefit the spirit. Like Mars, Saturn (known in the old days as "the greater malefic") is often too negatively described. If its energy is applied as discipline, hard work, patience, sustained effort, and the mature assumption of duties and responsibilities, however, it leads to genuinely earned and long-lasting success. Saturn builds a foundation for achievement in a professional way that lends stability to any endeavor. No surprise that he ruled over the Golden Age, and was Lord of the Seventh Heaven.

Saturn corresponds to virtues appreciated in the past (which is also ruled by Saturn), like prudence, thrift, loyalty, constancy, caution, and forethought. A serious energy characteristic of adulthood, it even better describes the wisdom of old age. One of Saturn's gifts, the ability to postpone gratification, is an indicator of emotional maturity. To quote 17th-century French author Jean de La Fontaine: "Patience and time do more than strength or passion."

In the body, Saturn is the skeletal structure upon which the entire body hangs. In the family, Saturn is the father who, as a wise and judicious parent, supports the child's growth and health while preventing harm. In wider society, Saturn is the government or "Establishment" that lays down the law, sets limits for individual freedom, and punishes transgressors. A naturally conservative energy, Saturn demands respect for tradition and authority.

But too repressive a regime becomes the negative patriarchy, harshly punitive and opposed to change. Saturn forgets that relentless emphasis on duty can kill spontaneity and creativity, that too much discipline can lead to rigidity, that too many heavy burdens can dampen enthusiasm and kill joy in life. Saturn's downside, it is true, is considerable. It can bring melancholy and pessimism in the face of delays or obstacles that seem insurmountable; depression and sadness at times of poverty or sterility; and bitterness and unhappiness in the face of misfortune. Saturn is deemed the Lord of Karma, bringer of inescapable challenges that seem fated.

On the other hand, worry or fear can either create difficulties or unnecessarily prolong existing ones. It takes great wisdom to discern whether a situation demands humble endurance— knowing that in the fullness of time, all shall pass—or positive action, sustained patiently in order to usher in slow change. Perhaps, as Martin Luther said, "The maturing soul is best watered by tears of adversity."

In esoteric lore, Saturn is *Rex Mundi*, the Lord of this World who tests the untried soul. He is also equivalent to the "ring-pass-not," the boundary that can be crossed only by the initiate who has gained the knowledge that allows admission to realms beyond the physical. (How appropriate that the physical planet Saturn is known for its rings!) As the last planet visible to the naked eye, Saturn symbolizes the limits of the ego and sense perception. Only by fulfilling his demands can you move into higher dimensions.

In alchemy, inner Saturn is "good gold," discovered after rejecting all that is superfluous. The Philosopher's Stone, which can heal all ills and bestow eternal life, comes from Saturn. In Jewish mysticism, Saturn's power to contract and narrow is *tzimtzum*, the self-constriction of God's light that allows creation to take place. Saturn is the crystallization of energy that allows the matter and form of our world to appear. It is also the alchemical process of the redemption of that matter and its restoration to light.

The Three "Modern" Planets

With the increasing use of telescopes in the 1700s, three other major planets were discovered. Since Saturn marks the bounds of both the ego and the known outer world, planets beyond it refer to realms beyond ordinary experience—precisely the ones to which Saturn prevents access until the soul is prepared. These planetary energies have been dubbed "transpersonal," relating to collective issues or long-term trends. In the individual horoscope, they may describe unusual abilities that are difficult to express or integrate into your life, or are late-blooming. All are charismatic and can destabilize both individuals and societies. For these reasons, the following discussions of their meanings are extensive.

URANUS (♅)

Uranus was first observed by William Herschel in 1781, and its discovery shocked both astronomers and astrologers. Here was an anomaly, a surprising and unexpected addition to the elegant system developed over several thousand years. Naming it Uranus (after some debate) rested on the logic that as Saturn was the father of Jupiter, so Uranus (Ouranos) was the father of Saturn.

Contemporary historian and writer Richard Tarnas has argued eloquently that Uranus' true nature is more like that of the Titan Prometheus.* In a Greek story of creation, Prometheus' brother Epimetheus was charged with the task of making humanity and alloting various gifts to animals and human beings. True to his name ("afterthought"), Epimetheus carelessly distributed everything to the animals, leaving human beings vulnerable. He begged his brother's help. Prometheus' brilliant solution was to steal the gods' fire to make humankind, now possessors of a divine spark, not only a match for, but superior to, the animals. Now human beings could stave off darkness and cold, make tools and weapons to defend themselves, and cultivate commerce and the arts.

The planet Uranus indeed seems to have much to do with fire. After it was discovered, astrologers sought to discern the type of events synchronous with its nature. An amusing story is told about water-colorist and ardent amateur astrologer John Varley (1778–1842). He became intensely interested in the newly discovered Uranus and made many observations of events coinciding with its aspects to other planets. One morning, on a day when Uranus was especially activated by Mars, Varley announced to his family that he intended to stay home all day, as something significant would happen. At noon, part of the house caught on fire. While others rushed

---

* Richard Tarnas, *Prometheus the Awakener: An Essay on the Archetypal Meaning of the Planet Uranus,* (Woodstock, Conn.: Spring Publications, c. 1995).

about throwing buckets of water on it, the delighted Varley sat down calmly to write about his discovery of the new planet's nature while his house burned to the ground.[*]

In keeping with its fiery nature, Uranus' symbol is sometimes the lightning bolt, literally bringing the light of heaven to Earth and illuminating dark terrain. Internally, it is sudden flashes of insight, moments of revelation, or spurts of creativity. New ideas break into the ordinary stream of thoughts, bringing innovative solutions to stubborn problems.

Uranus can also speed up the mind so that it bypasses logic and arrives at a conclusion by leaping from A to Z, bypassing intermediate steps. It fosters synthesis of unrelated elements to create something original. It is often intrigued by ideas outside the mainstream, seeking alternatives to conventional thinking. All esoteric studies—including astrology itself, alchemy, Kabbalah, the Norse runes, palmistry, and numerology—are in Uranus' domain.

Uranus is intrigued by mathematics and the sciences, which also use symbols to represent elements or processes that are experimental in nature. The planet includes anything related to electronics, computers, aviation, and robotics—whatever are the newest forms of technology—as well as science fiction (*Star Trek* and *Star Wars*).

Since all these unusual mental abilities, interests, and intellectual gifts are on a level beyond ordinary mental activity, Uranus is described as the "higher octave" of Mercury.

But Uranus' physical manifestations can be more mixed. Like lightning, Uranus is a shatterer, breaking into time and fracturing patterns. It is the pre-eminent energy of change—sudden, blinding, transformative. Though it may wish initially only to reform existing institutions, at an extreme it is the energy of revolution and rebellion seeking to liberate the imprisoned or oppressed. No surprise that at the time of its discovery, the American and French Revolutions were erupting in their respective countries. Uranus craves freedom and independence.

Uranus' dilemma is how to balance itself with Saturn, how to revitalize without destroying. Saturnian structures provide security

---

[*] James Herschel Holden, *A History of Horoscopic Astrology: From the Babylonian Period to the Modern Age,* (Tempe, Az.: American Federation of Astrologers, Inc., c. 1996), pp. 190–1.

and stability, but become rigid and life-inhibiting over time. Uranus breaks down the old and outworn to allow new life to flourish and new forms to appear. It is progressive by nature. It has been said that only Uranus can break the death grip of Saturn.

On a social level, the more rigidly Saturnian a society is, the more difficulty it will have with Uranian energy. Uranian types come in many varieties. They may be the intellectual elite, or they may be harmless eccentrics, unintegrated into society. They may be foreigners, strangers who come from outside. Though never fully integrated into the community, they may vitalize it by bringing contact with an alien culture. Uranians may also include the disabled, vagabonds, even freaks or anomalies of nature—anything different from the norm. (Read John Wyndham's *The Chrysalids* for a compelling story on this very theme.) Or they may be outsiders and anti-social fanatics, revolutionaries, those defiant of authority, who believe that only extreme measures will resolve social problems.

What does a culture do with those who do not look or behave like the majority? If the culture embraces Uranus, it will strive to be tolerant and accepting, to affirm social justice and equality before God and the law. A Uranian society will embrace altruism and idealism, and seek to include and integrate the oddball. The irony (and Uranus loves ironies, reversals, and inversions) is that Uranus prefers singularity and separateness. Literally, the planet itself is unique; it has a different motion from the others, being tilted 98 degrees on its axis and spinning from east to west.

Spiritually, Uranus represents the eruption of the divine into time. Uranus is the Great Awakener, disrupting your predictable life in this dimension. It reveals that the world is not as you see it, not as you think it, but is a constructed "reality." A Uranian-type experience can displace you in space and time, catapulting you back into the past or into an unfamiliar future. Such experiences can catalyze the remembrance of the divine spark within.

NEPTUNE (Ψ)

With Neptune's discovery in 1846, astrologers were faced once more with a new and unknown celestial body. Determining its nature was perhaps even more perplexing than establishing Uranus', because Neptune is most often connected with vagueness and confusion, with illusions and delusions. Astrological literature harps relentlessly on the difficulty of handling its energy.

The key to understanding Neptune is to realize that while Uranus breaks into our dimension to allow momentary flashes of insight into other realms of being, Neptune *is* those other realms of being. Neptune affirms not only that those realms exist and have as much "reality" as this one, but that your experiences of them have as much validity as those of the Saturn-bound world. Neptune is the spiritual truth that all forms are constantly changing shape, that they are ultimately evanescent, and that there is a unified Oneness behind them. Ultimately, the world dissolves and goes back into the many-named unknowable "somethingness" out of which it came.

These are mystical statements, upsetting to a materially oriented consciousness that believes only in data collected through the five senses. Neptune relies on sensitivities that tune into energies and not physical things, to subtexts and not words, to the essence behind the form rather than the form itself. It whispers its truths through the intuition, a direct knowing that bypasses logic. Neptune also reveals itself through the "sixth sense," in its varied manifestations as clairvoyance, clairaudience, and clairsentience.

Neptune is the psychic gift that allows perception of entities in the invisible dimensions: fairies and leprechauns, nature spirits, ghosts of the departed, spirits that have never been incarnate, angels and archangels. These so-called imaginary beings may have no more ultimate reality than physical ones, but they are fingers pointing toward the divine.

Pursuing a mystical path and aspiring to unity with the ultimate awakens the psychic sense. But teachers warn consistently against getting too distracted by or enamored of Neptune, for Neptunian entities are enchanters, luring the unwary as Vivianne trapped Merlin. Yet the stubborn persistence of strange and magical creatures in religious texts (like the Bible) and in fantastic literature (like *Lord of the Rings* or the Harry Potter books) may be a reflection of their existence on their own level and of our longing for the Infinite.

While Uranus may use the concentrated mind as a springboard to glimpsing Divine Mind (another name for the Godhead), Neptune uses the imagination. But it is controlled and focused, as in psychologist Carl Jung's technique of "active imagination." This involves visualizing and interacting with figures from dreams or daydreams to bring what was previously unconscious into the light to widen awareness and increase consciousness.

The best road map for exploring these amorphous dimensions is the Kabbalistic Tree of Life, a sophisticated and comprehensive model of the entire Universe, including both visible and invisible dimensions. Each of the ten centers on the Tree represents a level of being with clusters of associated ideas and images. The Tree provides the same type of structure for the inner worlds as Saturn does for the outer. By matching images to one of these centers, you can locate and comprehend your experience. Other representations that anchor spiritual seekers pursuing direct experience of the divine are Tibetan mandalas, Navajo sand paintings, and representations of the Christian City of God or the City Foursquare.

On the Kabbalistic Tree, Neptune may be associated with both Kether, the undifferentiated First Swirlings, and Yesod, the Treasure House of Images.* Yesod is traditionally linked to the Moon. In ancient times some ideas now attributed to Neptune would have been embraced by lunar symbolism. Neptune's primary symbol is the ocean, the amorphous greatness into which the individual soul, a mere drop of water, returns ecstatically at the end of a cycle.

To engage in mystical practices that open you to alternate levels of reality can be dangerous. You may have a vision of God or you may experience the primordial chaos before creation. Those who are unprepared risk emotional and mental imbalance, even madness. As with everything connected to the outer planets, their successful engagement depends on grounding in Saturn. Traditionally, this work has been reserved for those of a certain age (over forty in the Jewish tradition), who are deemed emotionally and mentally mature. Only those who have been prepared through faithful practice of spiritual disciplines, and determined to be psychically stable and completely ethical (having passed Saturn's initiations), may be successful at this.

There are very real pitfalls with Neptune. Instead of helping and healing, or offering a spiritually motivated service to others (bhakti yoga), you can become lost in a foggy world of fantasy and dreams (like the Land of the Lotus Eaters in the *Odyssey*). Instead of experiencing the ecstasy of the saint or the samadhi of the yogi, you can

---

* Editor's Note: Other Kabbalists ascribe Neptune to Chokmah, Pluto to Kether, and Uranus to Daath.

become addicted to alcohol or drugs (prescription or mind-altering), drowning in "spirits" instead of the Spirit. Instead of the refining and purifying element of Neptune, you can experience the polluted, the contaminated, the toxic. Instead of finding the reality of the intangible, you can substitute the glamor of the fleeting fad, the foolish longing of the romantic, or the projections of your own infantile longings.

Neptune is dubbed the higher octave of Venus, relating not to personal but to compassionate and unconditional love based on a soul connection. By extension, Neptune is the recognition of the World Soul.

The practical Neptune (a paradox!) may be the artist, one working especially in what I call the "intangible arts": music, theater, dance, poetry, and film, for these embrace rhythm and harmony and are relatively form-less. Where is the music when the instrument is laid aside? Where is the dance when the performer has left the stage? Where is the movie when the projector's light fades? Engaging art, as creator or appreciator, also offers grounding while exploring Neptune's realms.

PLUTO (♀)

When Pluto was first pinpointed in 1930, it was named for the Roman god of the underworld partly because its tiny body was far from the Sun's warmth in the darkness of deep space. Its status is currently in question. Is it an asteroid? A comet? A displaced moon of Neptune?

At the International Astronomical Union's annual meeting in 2006, a minority of attendees redefined Pluto as a "dwarf planet." However, more than seventy-five years of observation have convinced astrologers that Pluto is a factor to be reckoned with. It confirms the fact that powerful things sometimes come in small packages, however defined.

In view of the confusion concerning Pluto's identity, it is not surprising that Pluto has to do with unsolvable mysteries, with secrets, and with hidden dimensions of life that can never be fully explored or understood. It makes synchronistic sense that the god Pluto, when visiting the above-world, wore a helmet of invisibility.

The underworld is both the realm literally under the Earth's surface (containing caves, mines, buried treasure, graves) and the metaphoric internal "underworld" or realm of the unconscious (containing rich and unsuspected treasures of the human soul). Thus Pluto has to do with depth psychology as a whole—the use of such techniques as talk therapy or dreamwork to dredge up past traumas, dissipate energy trapped in complexes, work with obsessive/compulsive patterns, and bring release.

While Pluto can refer to the personal unconscious, in its impersonal aspect it also relates to the collective unconscious and most especially to the collective shadow. All that is rejected as useless, ugly, dirty, or downright evil is ascribed to it: garbage, slag, feces, waste. The underworld elements of society—criminals, spies, undercover detectives—all belong to Pluto. So do taboo and forbidden places or areas of life. So does all that frightens us: rats, spiders, demons, and dragons.

Pluto also has to do with the metallurgical process of refining (the "refiners' fire" mentioned in the Biblical book of Malachi) and with the alchemical process of the redemption of base matter and its transformation from dark to light substance. On the literal level of the physical body, Pluto has to do with the eliminative system.

Transformation is perhaps Pluto's most important keyword. Like the other two outer planets, it has to do with change. Plutonian change happens both subtly, through minute and progressive changes below the threshold of awareness, and dramatically, through events that erupt into history or into consciousness. Appropriately, Pluto rules earthquakes and volcanic activity.

This process of transformation can seem horribly destructive. You may experience dramatic crises or have to endure terrible suffering. Pluto rules cataclysms on a grand scale: not only earthquakes and volcanoes, but also extensive fires, famines, plagues, mass extermination, and world wars. Pluto is the embodiment of the destructive side of life—Shiva/Kali in the Hindu pantheon—an entirely necessary catabolism that complements birth and growth.

Something must die in order for something else to be born—although sometimes things just appear to die. While Saturn has more to do with the death of things that *stay* dead, with Pluto *what has been let go may resurrect itself and return in a glorified form.*

As a higher frequency of Mars, Pluto is about raw energy and will power, the concentrated and forceful (even ruthless) capacity to effect change in yourself or in the world. That may take the form of a sustained program of self-regeneration (through exercise, yoga, or diet) or an involvement in local, national, or international politics.

Exploration of magic, ritual, and the occult are Plutonian too, since mental exercises, visualizations, chanting, and verbal formulas are intended to alter your personal consciousness and to effect changes in the external world.

Since one form of power is money (a rich person is a "pluto-crat"), Pluto has to do with increasing your wealth through intelligent investing—and possibly, usually later in life (like Bill Gates and Warren Buffett), distributing it with the intention of improving society. Pluto can evolve from a drive to amass material things to a detachment that enables you to dispense with them. Such detachment frees you from the burden of managing your "stuff," allowing you to see more clearly and empowering you to act more wisely.

Many individuals touch Pluto in experiencing the power of sexual energy to create new life and to heighten consciousness (as in tantric yoga where it is a path to the divine). These potent experiences can bring healing—a healing that erases the memory of suffering you have endured before arriving at a place of peace.

Retrograde Planets

A planet is "retrograde" when it appears to be traveling backward through the sky. This is an optical illusion, similar to the experience of being in an express train passing a slower-moving local on a parallel track; the other train seems to be moving backward. Periodically, all planets (except the Sun and Moon, of course) appear to do this, because of the Earth's orbital position and speed in relation to other planetary orbits. The principal planets go through phases when they move ahead, become stationary, go retrograde, stop again, and move forward once more. Mercury does this three times a year for three weeks, while outer planets go retrograde for months.

In your chart a retrograde planet is indicated by the letter R or R_X next to it. Being retrograde can mean that the planet's energy is turned inward, slowed, and diverted from its usual paths. You have to rethink its expression or revisit ground previously covered. If, at the time of your birth, a planet was coming to a full stop before appearing to move either forward or backward, this slower motion adds special intensity.

CHAPTER TWO

The Signs: The Second Piece

In Mesopotamia and Egypt, the portion of the sky through which the Sun and the other planets apparently travel annually around the Earth was dubbed the *zodiac*. Of course, the Sun is not moving; Earth is. But astrology reflects life as we experience it from the perspective of living on Earth, the *geocentric* view. Planets other than the Sun travel eight degrees or more above and below the Sun's path, so the zodiac is a band of about sixteen degrees in width.

When the zodiac was determined in the first few centuries B.C.E., the signs and constellations coincided. But the tropical zodiac (based on Earth's seasons) is actually drifting slowly backwards against the backdrop of the heavens, moving at the rate of one degree every seventy-two years. The zero-degree Aries point now actually falls in the constellation of Pisces (hence we are in the "Piscean Age"), and will at some point in the near future contact the first star of Aquarius, ushering in the "Aquarian Age."

People disagree about the precise starting point of these ages, partly because of the uneven sizes of the constellations and partly because there are no definitive boundaries for them—just empty space between the last star of one constellation and the first star of the next. Some believe that the Aquarian Age is at least dawning, if not fully launched, given the remarkable scientific and technological developments of the last 150 years. One symbolic indication for this may be the shift in international power from military and commercial dominance at sea (Pisces) to the air (Aquarius).

Western astrologers measure the year from the point when the Sun crosses the celestial equator, around March 21st, which marks the beginning of spring and is called the Vernal Equinox. This creates a moving zodiac, a seasonal one (called tropical), rather than one fixed to the constellations (called sidereal).

The Greeks, who did the most to systematize astrological art and science, were a rational and intellectual people, and so divided the 360 degree band into twelve equal segments. The first thirty degrees of the annual seasonal zodiac beginning at the Vernal Equinox, regardless of the constellational degree, is the sign of Aries.

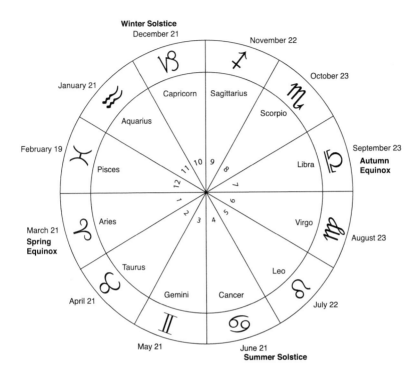

Figure 1. Signs of the Zodiac

The rest of the signs follow in zodiacal order: Taurus, Gemini, Cancer, Leo, Virgo, Libra, Scorpio, Sagittarius, Capricorn, Aquarius, and Pisces. The twelve thirty-degree segments became the solar "months," or "Sun signs" because the Sun travels through them each year at a predictable time. (See figure 1 above.)

Why twelve? The number twelve symbolizes the completion of a process in time, or totality in general: twelve Greek gods on Mount Olympus, twelve labors of Hercules, twelve tribes of Israel, twelve gems in the breastplate of the High Priest, twelve days of Christmas, twelve apostles, twelve gates into the Heavenly Jerusalem, and so on. Perhaps originally one person of each solar type was represented on a twelve-member jury, so that the full spectrum of human nature would deliver judgment in a court of law.

Twelve is also the product of four (the number of the world of *space*, as in the four cardinal directions, four points of the compass, the four winds) and three (the number of sacred *time* or of the three levels of the Universe). In alchemy, the four elements (earth, water, fire, and air) are multiplied by the three principles of sulphur, salt, and mercury. This mystical numerology turns up again in the division of earthly space, shown in the horoscope as twelve "houses."

Each sign became associated with a planet whose energy most comfortably matched it. So, for example, the Sun "rules" Leo, and the Moon "rules" Cancer; these bodies are most "at home" in their associated signs. Planetary rulerships are assigned around the zodiacal circle, starting from Leo and Cancer, by allotting the same planet to the next two signs on either side, in order of their sequence from the Sun. This means that Mercury rules both Gemini and Virgo, the adjacent signs, Venus the next two, and so on.

With the discovery of the outer planets, this neat system was challenged and the new planets were eventually ascribed to signs that shared a planetary ruler with another sign. Astrologers who practice "traditional" astrology continue to use the older rulerships; "modern" astrologers generally use the newer ones.

Like the planets, the signs are also archetypes represented by symbols like the crab, the bull, the twins, or two fish swimming in opposite directions. Perhaps this was a development of totemic relationships between clans or tribes and certain animals. Each sign portrays a pure personality type, with a number of typical characteristics both positive and negative. In actuality, of course, no individual is a pure type, since all ten planets are never in one sign at any given time.

These associations have accrued because every sign is a product of three rhythms superimposed on each other. The first is a double rhythm, that of yang and yin, or positive and negative polarities. Aries is masculine; Taurus is feminine, and so on. The second is a triple rhythm related to qualities of energy: cardinal or initiating energy, fixed or stabilizing energy, and mutable or changing energy. The third is a quadruple rhythm of the four elements. It is the basis for the theory of the four humors, whose proportions within the human body determine which of four basic temperaments a person exhibits.

Thus each sign is a unique blend of interacting energies embodying a combination of one, two, three, and four—the fundamental numbers, according to Pythagoras.

A further analogy between the greater and lesser, the heavenly and earthly, is the linking of each zodiacal sign to a part of the human body, starting with Aries at the head and ending with Pisces at the feet. This microcosmic man replicates the macrocosmic Man, called Adam Kadmon in Jewish mysticism and Perusha in Vedic cosmology. Practically, this scheme was used as a medical model to identify potentially weak organs, systems, or bodily functions, and to treat disease.

The Double Rhythm: Polarities
("And a one, and a two…")

This is the oldest dyad system known, also used as the basis for the Chinese I Ching. It divides the twelve signs into six alternating polarities. Odd-numbered signs are active, positive, masculine, and extroverted. Even-numbered signs are passive, negative, feminine, and introverted. Unfortunately, some undesirable associations have accrued to even-numbered signs because of gender bias. To avoid this, some astrologers refer to these polarities as yang and yin, terms borrowed from Chinese philosophy, emphasizing that both polarities are essential complements for wholeness. The significant point about double rhythm is outward versus inward orientation.

The Triple Rhythm: The Qualities or Crosses
("The Waltz of Time")

After the zodiacal circle is divided into four quadrants, a different quality of energy is assigned to the first, second, and third signs in each section. Thus Aries, Cancer, Libra, and Capricorn have a cardinal quality; Taurus, Leo, Scorpio, and Aquarius have a fixed quality; and Gemini, Virgo, Sagittarius, and Pisces have a mutable quality.

Cardinal energy is initiating and easily begins things. Fixed energy stabilizes, manages, and sustains what has been brought into being. Mutable energy loosens the structure and adapts what has been created to new and changing conditions. This classification may also refer to the three manifestations of the four elements in Hindu philosophy, called the *gunas* (activity, inertia, and harmony), and to the three manifestations of the Godhead (Brahma the Creator, Vishnu the Preserver, and Shiva the Destroyer).

Think of the qualities in relation to the seasons. The first month of spring brings the qualities of that season into being; the second month is its fullest flowering; the third sustains that flowering, but begins to make a transition to the next season.

		Table 1. Table of Rhythms			
SIGN	GLYPH	PLANETARY RULER	POLARITY (double rhythm)	QUADRUPLICITY (triple rhythm)	TRIPLICITY (quadruple rhythm)
Aries	♈	Mars	masculine	cardinal	fire
Taurus	♉	Venus	*feminine*	fixed	earth
Gemini	♊	Mercury	masculine	*mutable*	air
Cancer	♋	Moon	*feminine*	cardinal	*water*
Leo	♌	Sun	masculine	fixed	fire
Virgo	♍	Mercury	*feminine*	*mutable*	earth
Libra	♎	Venus	masculine	cardinal	air
Scorpio	♏	Mars/Pluto	*feminine*	fixed	*water*
Sagittarius	♐	Jupiter	masculine	*mutable*	fire
Capricorn	♑	Saturn	*feminine*	cardinal	earth
Aquarius	♒	Saturn/ Uranus	masculine	fixed	air
Pisces	♓	Jupiter/ Neptune	*feminine*	*mutable*	*water*

The Quadruple Rhythm: The Elements or Triangles ("The Box Step")

This divides the zodiacal circle into three segments of four signs, following an order of the four elements: fire, earth, air, and water. In a purely material sense, the elements refer to the four states of matter in the visible world: earth is solid; water is liquid; air is gas; fire is plasma or radiant ionized energy.

Yet the elements also encompass philosophical or esoteric meanings, and this is what they connoted to the ancients. They refer to four abstract levels of being: spiritual (fire), mental (air), emotional (water), and physical (earth). These also correlate to levels within the individual's aura. Fire is the etheric or vital body. Air is the mental or "causal" body attuned to universal mind. Water is the emotional or "astral" body, in which arise desires and emotional reactions. Earth is the physical body, which perceives material forms through the five senses. In Kabbalah, they are synchronous with the four worlds: Atziluth, Briah, Yetzirah, and Assiah.

The four visible elements all descend progressively from an invisible primary energy with many names: chi, prana, odic, or vital force. The Greeks called it "ether"; alchemists call it the "quintessence." Emanating from a pre-existing Oneness, the elements are experienced on the Earth plane as modes of being or ways of behaving, more subjective than objective.

THE ELEMENT OF FIRE: Fire's essential characteristic is the energetic exploration of life: to conquer, lead, and travel both physically and mentally. Key words are:
Positive: vital, extroverted, energetic, enthusiastic, inspirational, visionary, high-spirited, simple and direct in approach, physically active, dramatic, courageous
Negative: overly active to the point of burnout, restless, impatient, selfish, insensitive, willful, hasty, lacking in perspective, thoughtless, impulsive, reckless, extravagant, wild

THE ELEMENT OF AIR: Air is motivated to express thoughts in words to share information, interact with others, and influence society. Key words are:
Positive: focused on ideas and their expression, articulate, objective, mentally clear, detached, capable of forethought and understanding, socially adept and adaptable, cooperative, relational
Negative: unemotional and lacking in sympathy, impractical, "airheads," dissociated from the body and the physical world, over-adaptive, abstracted, glib and facile, hyperactive

THE ELEMENT OF WATER: Water is encouraged to experience emotions without repressing or being overwhelmed by them, achieve inner emotional security, and handle intuitive and psychic sensitivities adeptly (being both open and self-protective). Key words are:
Positive: deeply emotional, sympathetic and empathic, nurturing, calm and peaceful, sensitive, compassionate, imaginative, intuitive and even psychically aware
Negative: emotionally insecure and unstable, shy, timid, lacking in confidence, oversensitive, devitalized by fears with focus on negatives, easily influenced and manipulated, withdrawn and uncommunicative, vindictive and vengeful, takes everything personally, moody and depressed

THE ELEMENT OF EARTH: Earth seeks straightforward engagement with the physical world, mastery of it through efficient organization, and attainment of economic security, respect, and prestige due to hard work. Key words are:

Positive: practical, efficient, organized, realistic, patient, self-disciplined, hard-working, enduring and persistent, dependable, common-sensical, unpretentious, stable, a good sense of timing

Negative: slow and stodgy, lacking in vision, unimaginative, petty, excessively conventional, cautious so misses opportunities, narrow in perspective, stubborn, resistant to change, hoarding, ultraconservative

The Twelve Signs of the Zodiac

The double, triple and quadruple rhythms, when superimposed, generate qualities and associations correlated to the twelve signs. The following describes the essence of the signs imaginatively, personifying them as though they have a life and identity of their own. This actually facilitates chart interpretation later. (See figure 2 next page.)

Aries (masculine, cardinal, fire): The MOST yang and active of all fire signs. The most direct expression of the exuberant energy of life, Aries embodies the pure archetypal male as pioneer and warrior—often self-oriented and socially unsophisticated, but with admirable confidence and unchecked impulses urging you to engage, explore, assert.

Taurus (feminine, fixed, earth): The MOST yin of signs. Taurus takes on a physical body and is fertile and receptive to male seeding, but slow to respond, resistant to change, conservative regarding experiences and resources, and focused on establishing a stable and secure physical life rooted in one place.

Gemini (masculine, mutable, air): The first air sign. Gemini masters walking and talking, uses the five senses to explore the environment, and responds immediately in thought and speech—sometimes too quickly and superficially, but always changing to adapt to new information or new participants.

Cancer (feminine, cardinal, water): The first water sign. Cancer is deeply affected by early emotional experiences of childhood and early adolescence that set emotional and behavioral patterns, and strives to protect its inner sensitivity. It also has a maternal protectiveness capable of fierce action, tenaciously protecting the lives of

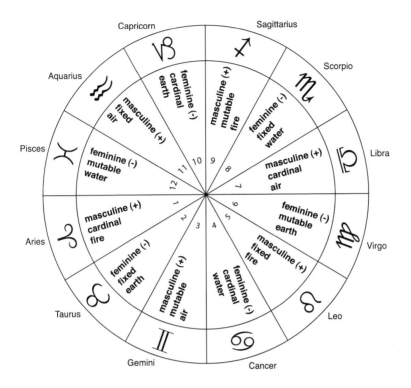

Figure 2. Triplicities of the Zodiac

those it loves: not only children, but the family as a whole, the tribe, the community, and the country.

Leo (masculine, fixed, fire): The second fire sign. Leo directs its energy to develop a genuine self-hood (presumably during adolescence), present that confident ego on the world stage, and take pride and find pleasure in the creative accomplishment that is the healthy expression of individual self-discovery.

Virgo (feminine, mutable, earth): The second earth sign. Virgo acquires skills and learning leading to a job, continually refining its efforts as the craftsperson does to develop technique leading to mastery within a chosen field. It finds security in offering practical, dependable service to an organization or a cause. Virgo uses its intellect critically to organize information clearly, accurately, and usefully, bringing order out of chaos.

Libra (masculine, cardinal, air): The second air sign. Libra seeks balanced exchange in one-on-one partnerships and marriage and harmony in groups, using diplomacy and tact to make social efforts more effective. It is motivated by a need to see justice done, and will negotiate for fairness and inclusiveness of every group represented within a community.

Scorpio (feminine, fixed, water): The second water sign. Scorpio works out the often hidden issues that arise from partnership, especially those related to shared resources or property due to needs for security and self-empowerment. Emotional focus is on the adult need to restrain emotions, while avoiding undue repression. The conflict predisposes to emotional energy buried in complexes, which then have to be released through intense therapeutic or transformative programs, or in creative pursuits.

Sagittarius (masculine, mutable, fire): The third fire sign. Sagittarius confidently and energetically explores the larger physical realm (through travel) and the mental realm (through reading or formal education) to gain knowledge. It pursues religion, philosophy, and metaphysics to discover the meaning of life, often changing focus as interests change.

Capricorn (feminine, cardinal, earth): The third earth sign. Capricorn is driven by a need for emotional and financial security, and is practically oriented to business and career success through hard work and self-discipline. It assesses the overall life achievement and the ultimate value of sacrifices made along the way. It may also wish to contribute to society once it has attained its goals.

Aquarius (masculine, fixed, air): The third air sign. Aquarius seeks to transform the culture or community through participation in clubs, groups, and organizations, or through charitable or volunteer work. Its intellectual efforts are marshaled to improve society, driven by altruism that seeks not only tolerance, but full social integration.

Pisces (feminine, mutable, water): The third water sign. Pisces strives to move beyond personal sensitivity into higher intuition, ultimately finding emotional security through discernment of spiritual realities spurred by some type of extra-sensory perception. Its attunement to higher dimensions can lead to creative expression of ideal forms or to compassionate service for the greater good.

Table 2. Table of Rulerships				
Planet	Ruler (very strong)	Detriment (weak)	Dignity/Exaltation (strong)	Fall (very weak)
Sun	Leo	Aquarius	Aries	Libra
Moon	Cancer	Capricorn	Taurus	Scorpio
Mercury	Gemini/ Virgo	Sagittarius/Pisces	Aquarius	Leo
Venus	Taurus/ Libra	Scorpio/Aries	Pisces	Virgo
Mars	Aries/Scorpio	Libra/Taurus	Capricorn	Cancer
Jupiter	Sagittarius/ Pisces	Gemini/Virgo	Cancer	Capricorn
Saturn	Capricorn/ Aquarius	Cancer/Leo	Libra	Aries
Uranus	Aquarius	Leo	Scorpio?	Taurus?
Neptune	Pisces	Virgo	Cancer?	Capricorn?
Pluto	Scorpio	Taurus	Aries?	Libra?

Notice that the first sign of each element is more personally oriented, the second expands the individual's interests into the greater community, and the third takes the individual into the maximally larger world.

Planets in Signs

Planets are symbols for cosmic realities that can no more be experienced directly than Semele could look directly at Zeus. When she tried, she was instantly destroyed, consumed by divine fire. Planetary energies are modulated to human consciousness through the medium of the signs. Like pieces of colored glass held before the eyes, signs filter planetary energy. Certain planets express themselves more or less easily through a particular sign; the energy of Mars, for example, is easily and dynamically expressed in Aries.

The most comfortable placement for a planet is in the sign that it rules. The next is in a sign deemed compatible, called being in "dignity" or exalted. In the sign opposite its rulership, a planet is said to be in "detriment" or disadvantaged. Opposite its dignified position, it has difficulty expressing itself or is in "fall." The table above illustrates this. (While they are included in the accompanying table, assignments of the newer planets are still being debated.)

When it comes to the actual interpretation of a chart, these traditional classifications can be modified by other factors. Such factors include connections that planets make to each other (called "aspects"), as well as their placement and strength in the horoscope for other reasons.

Planets' assignments to signs follow a pattern, starting with the Sun, probably assigned to Leo because August is the hottest month in the eastern Mediterranean, where the system coalesced. The Moon is then attached to Cancer, the sign next to it. Next, signs on either side of these two are given the same planetary rulerships, going around the wheel in opposite directions. Thus, Mercury rules both Gemini and Virgo (the adjacent signs), Venus rules the next two (Taurus and Libra), and so on. Careful reference to the Table of Rulerships will make this clearer.

Now we put can put together planetary energies and signs, and begin to speculate about how a planet will manifest itself in your psyche and life. **At this point, you may wish to obtain a copy of your own horoscope if you do not already have one, so that you can read about the following planetary placements in your own chart.** A number of websites will provide these for you free: a good one is *www.alabe.com/freechart/.*

The Sun in the Signs

The modern astrological community continues to debate whether the Sun-sign placement indicates already-developed talents you are born with, or whether it points to areas to be developed during your life. Consensus currently seems to favor the latter.

Your Sun placement shows your level of physical energy and your particular life purpose, expressing itself in the twelve signs as follows:

Sun in Aries: pioneering or self-asserting activities, with warmth and courage, but sometimes impulsively or in a way that overwhelms others. (Exaltation)

Sun in Taurus: establishing a comfortable, materially secure life through sustained effort and work within established and conventional spheres.

Sun in Gemini: pursuing a variety of activities that explore the mental realm in order to satisfy curiosity and gather information that can be communicated to others.

Sun in Cancer: sustaining familial and communal associations, establishing roots, and securing both financial and emotional security.

Sun in Leo: creative self-expression that draws others' attention and affection, and attests to the individual's dramatic talents and leadership capability. (Rulership)

Sun in Virgo: organizing information or environments to allow for the most efficient and productive use of energies and resources in service to a greater purpose.

Sun in Libra: balancing energies with another or with others, mediating or communicating in order to bring peace and harmony to human interactions. (Fall)

Sun in Scorpio: exploring the hidden or ill-understood aspects of life (power, sexuality, finances, the unconscious) in order to maximize resources, transform yourself or others, and release creative potential.

Sun in Sagittarius: exploring the world through the mind or through travel to expand your knowledge or awareness, and to appreciate its transmission through the ages as history, education, philosophy, or metaphysics.

Sun in Capricorn: achieving a level of success in the public sphere through hard work, self-discipline, and concentration, focusing on practical achievement, sometimes initially to the exclusion of other, more pleasureable pursuits.

Sun in Aquarius: connecting with others in friendship, and contributing to the improvement of society through participating in groups or organizations that have a social purpose. (Detriment)

Sun in Pisces: using your sensitivities in the helping and healing professions energized by compassion and a spiritually motivated desire to serve, or to be creative in the "intangible" arts (music, theater, dance, and film).

The Moon in the Signs

The Moon-sign placement reveals the individual's emotional needs and the manner of emotional expression. It expresses itself in the signs as follows:

Moon in Aries: volatility, quick to anger and to react. The emotions are instantly felt and immediately expressed so that they do not smolder. The individual is driven to find opportunities to initiate, to show courage, and to take a leadership role.

Moon in Taurus: stubbornness and resistance to argument and change. This is the most emotionally stable placement, needing predictability and security, both financial and emotional, and valuing quality and permanence. It is happiest in a calm and comfortable environment in which it can blossom. (Dignity)

Moon in Gemini: emotional changeability and fickleness. It needs to adapt continually to changing conditions, and is happiest when sharing thoughts and information and having the freedom to engage many varied circumstances.

Moon in Cancer: shyness and oversensitivity, and often taking things too personally. It needs emotional and financial security (often found through gaining or dealing in real estate); and is most comfortable when nurturing others by feeding or clothing them or providing them with a home. (Ruler)

Moon in Leo: ostentatious, grandiose, or egotistical; *or* devoted, magnanimous, and generous. It needs opportunities to shine, to achieve goals that contribute to an authentic sense of self. It is pleased with being in leadership situations in which it can share a grand vision or effect changes that reflect well on itself.

Moon in Virgo: subjects the emotions to rationality; consequently is perfectionistic, excessively critical, or fussy (like Felix in "The Odd Couple"). It needs neatness and order in its environment, and is most satisfied when its efforts to support an organization's efficient functioning are appreciated.

Moon in Libra: suffers when not in a partnership situation, whether personal or professional. It needs an other with whom to create a balanced relationship, or social encounters that are fun and harmonious. It is happiest when integrated within a social context or expressing its aesthetic sensibilities through some form of artistry.

Moon in Scorpio: a passionate and intense emotional nature. More than any other Moon placement, it is challenged to transmute negative emotions (resentment, vengefulness, hatred) into positive ones (forgiveness, unselfish love, compassion). It needs to overcome emotional repression by a gentle, steady release of feelings over time, especially by directing them into creative pursuits. It is happiest having achieved self-mastery through the healthy application of will power without excessive control. (Fall)

Moon in Sagittarius: restless, dissatisfied, and resistant to commitment; *or* charming, friendly, positive and optimistic, seeing life as humorous. It needs new worlds to conquer and new challenges to meet, as well as physical freedom. It takes pleasure in physical mastery of the body (as in sports) and the exploration of diverse physical environments or mental fields (in travel or study).

Moon in Capricorn: needs to watch for suppression of feelings or underdevelopment due to emotional shut-down. Emotional inhibition may originate in early childhood situations or negative parental influence. It needs meaningful work allowing disciplined efforts to achieve position and rewards, leading to a more secure sense of self. It is happiest with steady accomplishment of practical goals, and through being recognized as a productive member of society. (Detriment)

Moon in Aquarius: emotionally cold and detached, often because of over-control of feelings through intellectual domination or emotional trauma. It needs to allow feelings to surface, and show its clearheaded, broadminded outlook in the broader social milieu. It is happiest expressing altruism and idealism through efforts to improve society, to relieve suffering, and to bring groups together.

Moon in Pisces: extremely sensitive and overly responsive; has difficulty establishing boundaries and feeling grounded without resorting to escapist outlets like drugs, fantasy, or alcohol. It needs to be engaged in helping or healing work where a genuine spiritual motivation energizes its service, or engaging artistic pursuits. It is happiest fulfilling its ideals through service in psychically clear surroundings.

Mercury in the Signs

Mercury's sign placement reveals the way the mind functions, possible intellectual interests, and overall style of communication. It expresses itself in the signs as follows:

Mercury in Aries: sharp and concise. It sees the point of a debate or argument quickly, and responds in the same way, directly and honestly, perhaps impatiently or with wit or sarcasm.

Mercury in Taurus: conservative, carefully weighs options before responding, so that sometimes the opportunity for exchange has passed. It perseveres in applying the mind logically (and not abstractly) to practical problems with great common sense.

Mercury in Gemini: quick and has great curiosity, sometimes with a mischievous or humorous take. Easily articulate and verbally sophisticated, it enjoys verbal games and puns. It may seem excessively talkative or inconsistent, jumping to conclusions or skipping over facts, or avoiding hard research. (Ruler)

Mercury in Cancer: highly aware of the emotional overtones of speech and words' effect on others; tries to be kindspoken. Thinking can be empathic. It may have a good memory, but difficulty forgetting negative experiences. Thought processes may be influenced by moods and consequently changeable.

Mercury in Leo: a dramatic flair and confidence, used to persuade others of the rightness of its ideas or to enlist their enthusiasm for projects. It can approach problems creatively, but is uninterested in fine points. Ideas may be self-referential, and it may enjoy displaying knowledge in order to impress others, seeming intellectually superior. (Fall)

Mercury in Virgo: logical and methodical, with a well developed intellectual capability easily applied to business or science. With a discriminating intelligence and gifts of conciseness, precision, and clarity, it makes admirable critics and first-rate problem-solvers. It enjoys organizing information and solving intellectual puzzles. It is the best placement for dealing well with details within a larger context. (Ruler)

Mercury in Libra: gives a fair and balanced assessment of opposing points of view, though it may lose sight of its own opinion in the process. It can express itself charmingly and diplomatically, with an aesthetic appreciation for language and rhetoric. It may be too easily persuaded by others, and may see so many different perspectives on an issue that it becomes overwhelmed and indecisive.

Mercury in Scorpio: strategically, deliberately uses the mind as a tool of persuasion or propaganda, penetrating others' motivations to convince them more effectively. This is the mind of the researcher, the prober of mysteries, or the discoverer of hidden secrets, so it is an asset in the chart of a PR person, detective, investigative journalist, or gossip columnist. It is also capable of being ironic, cynical, or cutting, and may go silent, withholding information to create an aura of mystery.

Mercury in Sagittarius: pursues many and varied interests in the search for truth, sometimes scattered or easily distracted. The mind has a philosophical cast, often ignoring facts or details in favor of the grander view. It can seem a know-it-all, but its optimistic outlook can restore others' lost faith. It can speak without thinking, the classic "foot-in-mouth" syndrome. (Detriment)

Mercury in Capricorn: focuses on material realities and the practical solution of problems. This is the mind of a businessperson or engineer. In using language in a serious, methodical, and unimaginative way, it may not consider the emotional impact of words on others. Its strength is in being realistic; its drawback is in being humorless.

Mercury in Aquarius: brilliant and insightful, concerned with ameliorating social ills and capable of grasping ideas ahead of their time. An independent thinker, it may alternate between being flexible and inflexible in thinking. It can think both spontaneously and circumspectly. While it can be creative, open-minded, and tolerant, and has the best talent for thinking abstractly and creating syntheses of all the signs, it can also get lost in abstraction or appear arrogantly certain of the rightness of its own ideas. (Dignity)

Mercury in Pisces: imaginative and intuitive, with sensitivity to the feeling tone of words rather than their precise literal meaning. It uses language to create images, in a poetic way, with an insouciance about the truth or reality of what it creates. It can be almost telepathic in its ability to tune into another's thoughts, but may be inarticulate in expressing its own. (Detriment)

Venus in the Signs

Venus's sign placement has to do with how the individual attracts love and appreciates beauty and the arts. It tells of the capacity for relatedness in intimate connections or with friends in a wider social context. It expresses itself in the signs as follows:

Venus in Aries: passionate and assertive in relationships, going after what it wants but not always sensitive to how it is received, or to another's needs. Passion may be short-lived. It likes to take the lead in social situations. (Detriment)

Venus in Taurus: strong, with an innate sensual appreciation of beauty and luxury that gives it genuine artistic potential. It is loyal and faithful in friendships, and takes commitments seriously. It appreciates physical closeness (hugs from friends, and regular and passionate sexual relations with lovers). It can be possessive and jealous and does not let go easily. (Ruler)

Venus in Gemini: changeable, delighting in many and varied social contacts, but sometimes reluctant to commit, preferring to play the field. It can be successful in partnering if variety and amusements characterize the relationship. Considered fickle and unreliable, its aesthetic preferences change quickly too. It may be charming and comfortable in social situations and knows how to flirt!

Venus in Cancer: sensitive to friends' and partners' needs; enjoys providing a home and both emotional and physical nurturance. With a romantic streak, it stays committed, in part because of a high need for emotional security. It is also possessive, and has difficulty letting go. Partners may feel crowded if it hovers too much. It can be socially shy, preferring to be where it feels safe.

Venus in Leo: loves the drama of relationships, and enjoys attention from partners and friends. It likes to be generous and magnanimous, though it may expect the partner to play a secondary, supportive, and adoring role. With an attractive warm personality, it can be very charismatic. It may appreciate partners for their appearance, and so attract "arm candy." In love, it may be demonstrative, but not always genuine in expressing feelings.

Venus in Virgo: analyzes partners' strengths and weaknesses, and is discriminating in choice of friends. The most emotionally self-sufficient of signs, it may choose to be alone or to have a small number of reliable friends. It shows love through practical service to the partner and by being helpful and faithful. (Fall)

Venus in Libra: a strong need for an equal partner with whom to share feelings and ideas, and a wide network of friends and acquaintances leading to an active social life. A strong aesthetic sense enables the creation of beautiful environments or pleasant social occasions. It may over-analyze relationships and suffer from disharmony in them. (Ruler)

Venus in Scorpio: intense and passionate, attracting partners through magnetic sexual attraction or seduction. It is deeply sexual and longs for the deathless and faithful love of Romeo and Juliet, or Heloise and Abelard. It may exploit partners for monetary or social gain, and has difficulty achieving a balance of power. If thwarted or insecure, it can be jealous, possessive, or manipulative, and needs to transform negative emotional responses or actions to be harmless and loving. (Detriment)

Venus in Sagittarius: enjoys a variety of social contexts and many intellectually stimulating people. It may over-idealize or reject partners who are not honorable or equally idealistic. Its primary need is for space, so it may be involved with nobody or with more than one partner, especially from a distance. A typical "Peter Pan," it shies away from adult commitments and may avoid confrontations or be uncomfortable with intimacy.

Venus in Capricorn: connects with a partner for status, security, or economic reasons, and then dutifully fulfills the role of partner or parent. It can demonstrate a profound, serious, and committed love, or sideline emotions for more practical considerations, afterward feeling the lack of love acutely. It warms to others slowly, and may experience a long-lasting and faithful love later in life.

Venus in Aquarius: needs a high degree of change, intellectual stimulation, and freedom in relationships, which may be socially unconventional. It can have a wide social network, not always with deep emotional bonds, but often sharing similar ideas or passion for causes. It may have unusual or eccentric ideas about romantic or sexual relationships.

Venus in Pisces: in love with Love. This most idealistic and romantic of signs has difficulty accepting imperfect humanness, and may be more comfortable with love as an ideal, love of the arts, or love of God. While it can be devoted and self-sacrificing, it must beware of escaping into romantic fantasies or having its good nature exploited. (Dignity)

Mars in the Signs

The Mars placement reveals the energy quality and the sphere it most energizes. It shows how people go after what they want, what their sexual energy and style may be, and how the male side of the psyche may be described. In a woman's chart, it is one of the factors suggestive of the type of man she attracts; in a man's chart, it reflects the male image he tries to emulate. It expresses itself in the signs as follows:

Mars in Aries: strong, with clear intention and direct movement toward goals; takes action physically with a heroic courage that overrides restraints. Energy rises quickly and impulsively, but may be short-lived, impatient, reckless, even brutal. It may be easily excited and vigorous, and the sexual style is competitive and conquering. (Ruler)

Mars in Taurus: slow but patient, applies energy to practical accomplishments. It is capable of sustained effort over time, is better at defense than offense, and may control the temper for a long time before finally exploding. Sexually, it is deeply sensual and passionate, though passive and indulgent. (Detriment)

Mars in Gemini: quick, though easily defused or distracted, so efforts may not be sustained due to scattering. It can be verbally assertive and quick-witted, and enjoys debates and arguments. It may talk its way out of difficulties or use humor to defuse situations. It can be stimulated through words and kept intrigued through variety, but is sometimes inclined to talk rather than act.

Mars in Cancer: indirect, has difficulty asserting due to sensitivity and empathy with others. Emotions affect commitment to projects, so it may alternately take action or be paralyzed. If it does not feel secure and emotionally comfortable, it may be shy and sensitive in sexual encounters. (Fall)

Mars in Leo: bold and daring, driven by visionary zeal or creative inspiration to act with grand gestures. It can be direct and persistent in achieving goals, but may be impractical and ungrounded or let wounded pride interfere with progress. It is self-confident, aware of performing with flair, and loves attention as the "courtly lover."

Mars in Virgo: methodical and precise, with energy oriented to practicalities and capable of skilled or routine work sustained over time. It may lose energy by over-focusing on details or be hesitant due to perfectionism or self-doubt. It is sexually discriminating to the point of avoiding partners who lack manners or skimp on personal grooming, but is capable of quiet, sustained passion.

Mars in Libra: indecisive, with difficulty asserting by being too ready to listen to opposite arguments or to compromise. Energy goes into mental levels, so it may use negotiating tactics or charm to avoid conflict, while talking itself out of taking a stand. It tries to be fair in love and war, and so may annoy a partner by dithering over opportunities or being reluctant to engage in unaesthetic actions. (Detriment)

Mars in Scorpio: passionate, uses strategy to achieve its purposes, motivated by powerful emotions to use energy in transforming itself, others, or the environment. Persevering, it may have difficulty adjusting course or moderating its power drive, and may be tempted to use underhanded methods to achieve goals. Sexually, it is deeply erotic and seductive, drawn to exploring sexual taboos. (Ruler)

Mars in Sagittarius: puts enthusiasm into many and varied activities that change frequently, especially those pursuing ideals or exploring new territory, both physical and mental. This is the athlete, or the crusader or missionary who angers more easily over causes or principles than personal issues. Sexually, it is quick to desire, but inclined to restlessness and a need for freedom.

Mars in Capricorn: uses concentration and determination to gain materially, even if opposed. Energy is disciplined and persistent, responsibly directed toward constructive achievements. The sexual drive can be controlled or separated from the emotions, but is strong and steady. (Dignity)

Mars in Aquarius: changeable on the mental plane, eager to communicate ideals to inspire or persuade others to action. It is fascinated by theories and unusual ideas, but may not see their practical application, though it may try to force its opinions on others. It inclines to independent, erratic, and oblique action. Friendship is a basis for connection, with an unconventional and experimental approach to sex that it may redirect periodically into intellectual pursuits.

Mars in Pisces: fluctuates with the emotional flow. It can act on others' behalf or for spiritual principles, but has difficulty with self-assertion. It may act on instinct or indirectly, often winning by passively submitting or turning the other cheek. It can be a romantic, tender, and sensitive lover, but caught up in fantasies or too easily seduced.

Jupiter in the Signs

Jupiter takes longer to circle the Sun than planets like Venus, which may traverse a sign in less than a month, or Mars, which may stay in one sign for six weeks. Jupiter spends, on average, *an entire year* in a sign, taking twelve years to complete its orbit. Interpretations of Jupiter and the planets beyond it thus apply to a sizable peer group and may be less personally specific.

Jupiter's sign placement points to what people idealize; how they search for meaning through religion, philosophy, or metaphysics; how they seek to learn and grow by engaging new spheres, especially ones leading to greater knowledge, understanding, and expanded awareness. It also indicates where people can overdo or go to extremes. It expresses itself in the signs as follows:

Jupiter in Aries: idealizes personal freedom and assertiveness, and learns through physical activity and taking risks. With a high level of physical energy and confidence, it may espouse a philosophy of self-reliance. Motivations are very personally oriented.

Jupiter in Taurus: holds pleasure and comfort as ideals. It values stability and is philosophically conservative and stoic, learning through hands-on practical experience. It may desire to accumulate more materially or expand its sensual exploration of the world.

Jupiter in Gemini: values the compulsive amassing of information in a quest to know and understand more. It increases mental activity, doubting and questioning constantly, and may focus on knowledge that has only short-term use or is superficial. (Detriment)

Jupiter in Cancer: values security, family, stability, and loyalty to clan and country. It learns through emotionally motivated exploration, and can help and support others. Growth comes through nurturing and compassion. (Exaltation)

Jupiter in Leo: values opportunities to lead, therefore being in a position to help others by being magnanimous and generous. Learning has a personal cast, and while ideals and principles can be genuine motivators, it may be distracted from study by luxury, ease, and show.

Jupiter in Virgo: values order and organization in the fulfilment of practical objectives. Idealism may be challenged by subjecting ideals to intellectual examination or deflating them through cynicism. It may not accept a philosophy wholeheartedly because of feeling intellectually superior or being overly critical. (Detriment)

Jupiter in Libra: values cooperation, leading to peace and harmony in society, and justice and fairness before the law. It may do this by using knowledge and skilled communication, the mind being the chief vehicle for growth. One of the most idealistic placements, it may seek the ideal relationship, the ideal learning situation, or the ideal aesthetic experience through the arts.

Jupiter in Scorpio: values power that comes from controlling emotions and self-projection, and from success due to persistent dedication to goals. It learns through releasing emotions, channeling them into creative pursuits or explorations of psychology, finances, or the secrets of life and death.

Jupiter in Sagittarius: values noble ideals like honesty or honor. It seeks to grow through wide-ranging religious and philosophical explorations, and by literally traveling. More than most, it wants to improve, learn more and gain wisdom through an enthusiastic search for truth. (Ruler)

Jupiter in Capricorn: values practical efforts to increase material prosperity or consolidate worldly position. Values are conservative: hard work, fulfillment of duty, playing a defined role within established structures. Cautious and pragmatic—even pessimistic—it may distrust philosophies and religions, and rely too much on self and the concretely visible. (Fall)

Jupiter in Aquarius: values "liberty, equality, and fraternity," the Aquarian Age Utopian ideals of brotherly love, and freedom and democracy. It grows mentally, being especially open to new ideas, and has the unique ability to weigh theories impersonally, though it can get lost in abstract intellectual speculation, as well as be superficial and impractical.

Jupiter in Pisces: values compassion, forgiveness, and unselfish love, as well as service to the divine. Emotions energize a search for direct religious or mystical experience that may lead to inner peace and wisdom. En route, it must watch being gullible or exploited. (Ruler)

Saturn in the Signs

Saturn takes, on average, *two and a half years* to travel through a sign, and so marks an even broader peer group. Still, its placement acutely reveals personal vulnerabilities or external limitations that can be overcome over time with patient sustained effort and a mature attitude.

Of all the planetary placements, Saturn speaks most tellingly of significant lessons to be learned, as well as wisdom to be gained— only possible in this dimension. No wonder it is dubbed "The Lord of Karma." The key to overcoming Saturnian problems is the resolution of issues *internally* first, rather than looking for changes externally.

The element of Saturn's placement is in itself significant and worth separate consideration before delineating Saturn's expression in individual signs.

Saturn in fire signs: can dampen enthusiasm and inhibit efforts due to self-doubt or a feeling that taking action is useless. Careful preparation and consideration of outcomes, along with sustained energy and will power channeled into meaningful areas, can lead to achieving personal goals.

Saturn in earth signs: initially may have trouble dealing with practical earthly concerns, such as finding meaningful sustained work, building financial security, and handling money and resources. Patiently accepting the slowness and limitations of this dimension, along with common sense, wise and efficient use of time and energy, and becoming organized can lead to practical mastership.

Saturn in air signs: can feel insecure about the level of knowledge or intellectual abilities, and can overcompensate by becoming a know-it-all or the expert with many degrees. Challenging negative thoughts and replacing them with positive ones (in the style of Albert Ellis' Rational-Emotive Therapy) can evolve into objective and detached consideration of issues, with disciplined and concentrated thought leading to unusually clear and coherent communication. One literally "masters the mind."

Saturn in water signs: can be blocked in emotional expression because of fear, hypersensitivity, or deep insecurity resulting from poor parenting or past traumas. Inner strength, emotional balance, and self-sufficiency can be cultivated by letting feelings gently surface over time and by conscious and consistent self-nurturing. This develops eventually into the capacity to express genuine feelings in a deeply felt and caring way.

Now we can be more specific about Saturn's effect in each sign. Initially Saturn inhibits the free expression of a sign's potential or may incline toward defensively overdoing things in inauthentic ways to compensate for feelings of inferiority or fear. Saturn insists on developing a sign's genuine qualities over time. Saturn expresses itself in the signs as follows:

Saturn in Aries: has difficulty being self-assertive, expressing masculine qualities, or feeling confident. The challenge is to overcome a sense of inadequacy by developing a healthy ego that can take the initiative and easily handle life's conflicts. (Fall)

Saturn in Taurus: inhibits the enjoyment of sense-based pleasures and has increasing fears of losing material security or possessions. The challenge is to generate the confidence to enjoy what the world has to offer, despite recognizing the inevitability of change, after developing inner security based on a genuine sense of self-worth.

Saturn in Gemini: frustrating early learning experiences, limiting intellectual exploration and dampening natural curiosity, makes them underachieve or be silent through fear of showing ignorance or being wrong. Developing language skills—to the point of examining each individual word—and weighing thoughts lead to communicating with maturity, authority, and intellectual depth.

Saturn in Cancer: childhood wounding from lack of love or emotional support can reveal itself in hypersensitivity, enmeshment with or emotional distance from family, extreme self-protectiveness, and an emotional neediness and hunger leading to literal overeating or accumulating material things (especially land or real estate). Gently releasing deeper feelings, building genuine emotional security through trusting emotions, instincts and intuitions, and seeing the larger Universe as a source of support create emotional maturity and an ability to nurture oneself and others. (Detriment)

Saturn in Leo: an inauthentic and showy self that deeply fears being unloved, disrespected, and undignified; is reluctant to display its creative products. Through developing a secure sense of self-worth grounded in Self instead of ego, it gains the confidence to have fun in life, dare to love, and be consistently and successfully creative. (Detriment)

Saturn in Virgo: works through perfectionism and workaholism, motivated by fear of criticism, being inadequate, or feeling useless, to achieve a healthy balance of relaxation and meaningful work seen as service to the whole. Saturn here must also focus on the role of thought and attitude in generating good health in an efficiently functioning body that is cared for and appreciated.

Saturn in Libra: fears loss of identity in personal relationships, so delays commitments until it has evolved a stronger sense of self and developed interpersonal skills, like responsible and fair cooperation, negotiation, and decision-making. Saturn here leads to greater decisiveness in thought and action and to wise application of ideals to human interactions. (Dignity)

Saturn in Scorpio: fears loss of internal psychic balance due to intense emotions or loss of autonomy by being controlled or manipulated by others, generating compulsive use of others as defensive self-protection or compensation for a sense of loss or lack. Moderating passions, appreciating the power of surrender, allowing crucial life experiences to effect change, trusting inner strength to meet challenges, and deepening intimacy to experience profound sexual satisfaction all lead to greater emotional satisfaction.

Saturn in Sagittarius: moves from defensive positions of skepticism and cynicism or unthinking reliance on authority, with accompanying intolerance or judgmentalism, through crises of faith to developing an enduring, wise, and meaningful philosophy about the divine and human worlds. This position brings a healthy mental discipline to potentially naive and scattered thinking.

Saturn in Capricorn: fears the inability to generate material prosperity or be respected by society for perceived success, leading to overwork and a severely limited life. The solution is to cultivate confidence in handling positions of responsibility and to trust that hard work, patience, and efforts for the betterment of the community will ultimately bring recognition. (Ruler)

Saturn in Aquarius: fears that their ideas will be ignored or considered too eccentric, or fears new ideas in general and so is intolerant and mentally controlling. Tempering radicalism and tolerating diversity leads to the practical application of well-thought-out and innovative ideas that may be embraced by society and catalyze social transformation. (Ruler)

Saturn in Pisces: fears engaging physical life and handling material affairs, leading to defensive withdrawal from the world; tries to escape emotional pain or lack of meaning through drugs, alcohol, or unhealthy relationships; and allows victimization or exploitation due to low self-esteem or loss of boundaries. Using empathy, intuition and psychic impressions as guides (rather than authoritarian teachers or rigid dogma) and embracing a spiritual discipline that grounds personal identity in the soul and recognizes the oneness of all life give emotional strength, provide practical outlets for compassion that help relieve the world's suffering, and lead to inner experiences of peace and serenity.

The Outer Planets in the Signs

Uranus spends approximately seven years in a sign, Neptune fourteen, and Pluto between twelve and thirty-two. They mark not only generations, but also artistic, social, and historical trends. Because of their long stay in one sign, their meanings are more collective than personal. It is their placements in houses and their aspects to personal planets that individualize their meanings for you.

CHAPTER THREE

Houses: The Third Piece

W<small>E NOW HAVE A PICTURE OF THE COSMOS</small>, with the planets appearing to circle Earth against the backdrop of the signs of the zodiac. We have a long-developed conceptual system with amplified meanings of planets and signs, applying to vast numbers of people. But at this point, we have no way of individualizing these patterns to capture each person's uniqueness. To do this, we have to discover a way of "bringing heaven down to Earth."

Creating an Individual Chart

An individual chart represents a snapshot of the heavens, with the planets in various positions in their orbits, from a specific geographic location at a particular moment—the moment of birth. This snapshot becomes a personal horoscope, in which the grander picture of the cosmos reveals the individual's life and purpose.

This picture reflects the view of an observer at a given place on Earth—which means Earth is at the center of the chart. Astrologers use a geocentric (Earth-centered) perspective to reflect common daily experience. The Sun is, of course, the center of our solar system, but a heliocentric (or Sun-centered) model would only be useful to someone living on the Sun.

Putting this model on paper is the greatest challenge for astrologers, perhaps reflecting the philosophical and spiritual conundrum of how a soul manifests in a time-space dimension. The challenge of transferring a three-dimensional picture to a flat two-dimensional representation is a problem in spherical trigonometry and geometry. Any such model, just like any map, contains distortions.

Let's start with the ecliptic, the apparent path of the "chariot of the Sun" through the heavens. The Sun arcs across the sky and intersects the local horizon, the place where we are most anchored on Earth. This connects the wheeling of the cosmos with the turning of the world on its axis—the greater with the lesser. The point in the east where the Sun rises is called the Ascendant.

The local horizon is also envisioned as a circle, separated into a visible half-sphere (above the horizon) and an invisible one (below the horizon). It goes "as far as the eye can see," from east to west, where the Sun, Moon, and other planets appear to rise and set on a daily basis. Planets below the horizon are not visible to the naked eye, but are still included in the birth chart.

The Earth rotates on its axis one complete revolution every day—though from our perspective, it looks as if the zodiac is turning around us, rising at the Ascendant and setting at the Descendant. The zodiac rises in the east very rapidly—much faster than any of the planets, even the Moon. Every four minutes, the next degree of the zodiac appears to come up over the horizon. Some astrological computer programs allow you to watch this moment by moment, as planets rise and ascend in the sky.

The faster a planet or a point (like the Ascendant) moves through the zodiac, the less likely it is to be the same in someone else's chart, therefore, the more individual it is. So it is logical to use the Ascendant as the chart's beginning point. This allows the universal to become personal and shows how the positions of the signs and planets translate into specific life circumstances and events.

The Ascendant is the entry point for constructing a horoscope, so it is analogous to the sign Aries, the primary symbol of the "beginning of things." Since the Ascendant is where the heavens meet our physical space (Earth)—and where the Sun first appears at the day's dawn—it reflects Aries-like qualities that go with the first eruption of any physical thing into time: a forceful, assertive, and energetic temperament.

Just as we divided the yearly cycle into twelve parts, the solar months, we also divide the twenty-four hours of day and night into twelve time periods called "houses." This division of earthly space into twelve sectors indicating different areas of life parallels *all* twelve signs of the zodiac, starting with Aries at the Ascendant and going counterclockwise around the chart. The house system is not an exact equivalent of the zodiac system, as there are subtle differences. But overlaying the yearly pattern on the daily pattern is another way of relating the greater to the lesser.

The first house is the "natural" house of Aries, and has Arien meanings and associations attached to it. This development in astrology began a long time ago, probably sometime in the mid 2nd century B.C.E., and is attributed to the Egyptian priest-astrologer

Petosiris. It is first fully described by the famous Claudius Ptolemy of Alexandria, whose astrological writings, especially the *Tetrabiblos*, became the basic texts of astrology for 1500 years.

The simplest way to calculate the houses is to divide the 360 degrees of the zodiac into twelve equal segments of thirty degrees each, starting at the Ascendant. This is called the "Equal House" system, and is the one Ptolemy used. The resulting picture will show a wheel with twelve spokes radiating out from the center (in this case, Earth), like a neatly cut-up pie. The horizon is the horizontal diameter formed by two of the spokes (radii) of the circle across the center of the image. These spokes are extremely important, as they are two defining "angles" of the horoscope.

The Angles

The four angles of the horoscope are derived from the four horizontal and vertical spokes. These primary cross-shaped angles establish the framework for the entire chart. They correspond to the position of the Sun at sunrise, noon, sunset, and midnight. These are the four most important divisions of the day cycle, and so have special symbolic import. (See figure 3 on opposite page.)

The **Ascendant**, the degree of the ecliptic rising in the east, is always to the center-left of the chart. Planets lurking around this point are "rising," and the sign on the Ascendant is the "rising sign." This is also the beginning or "cusp" of the first house, and the point of contact with your local environment, your "window on the world."

The meaning of the Ascendant relates to meanings given to the first house. Many consider the Ascendant analogous to psychologist Carl Jung's concept of the "persona," the "mask" or socialized self with a particular style of self-presentation. Just as planets ascending above this point are becoming visible, so this point represents the birth or appearance of the individual in the world. It also has to do with the image you project of yourself, the impression you make on others, the way you take action in the world, and the lasting effect you have on your environment. It corresponds to others' perception of your "personality."

It is vitally important to have a precise birth time to determine an accurate Ascendant. Generally, the astrologer wants the moment when the baby first breathes, which is its beginning as an independent entity. This is often not the recorded birth time, which can easily

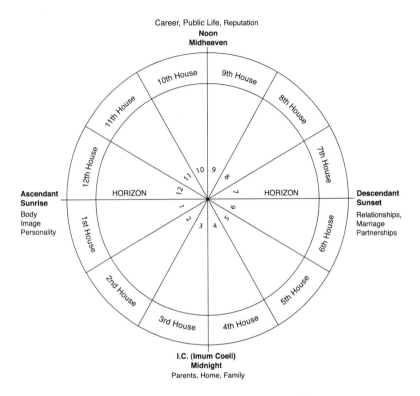

Figure 3. The Four Angles

be off by five or ten minutes. Every four minutes, the degree on the Ascendant changes, advancing through each degree of the sign. This affects the interpretation in noticeable as well as subtle ways, so the more precise the birth time, the clearer the picture, and the more potentially accurate the delineation.

The *Descendant* is always exactly 180 degrees opposite the Ascendant, to the center right of the chart. Planets here are "setting." Its meaning is directly related to the description of the seventh house, the house of "the other," as opposed to the first house, which is about you. The Descendant has to do with the way others act toward you, and their impact on you. It also describes your close associations and what you attract in others, especially in marriage, long-term committed relationships, or business partnerships.

The **Midheaven** or MC (short for *medium coeli,* Latin for "middle of the heavens") is at the top of the chart, about where the Sun would be at noon. This point is determined by establishing where the ecliptic (the path of the Sun) crosses the local meridian. This is the place in the sky perpendicular to the horizon, where the Sun (or any other planet) reaches its highest point in the sky, a place of maximum visibility. Just as the Sun dominates the sky at midday, planets at this point have a powerful presence and are said to be "culminating."

The significance of the Midheaven is derived from meanings attributed to the tenth house, although in some house systems the Midheaven and the beginning point of the tenth house do not always coincide. This is the place of greatest extension of self into the larger world of career and public life. It relates to your career, reputation, and social status.

The *IC* (*imum coeli,* or "lowest heaven") is directly opposite the MC, at the bottom of the chart. Its meaning is derived from meanings for the fourth house, profoundly related to the foundations of your life supporting your public achievement (tenth house), including ancestors, parents (perhaps especially the mother), and current family, as well as home and real estate that may provide basic security.

All twelve signs of the zodiac appear to rise, culminate, set, and cross the bottom of the chart during the twenty-four hours of the day, so you can have any one of the thirty degrees of any of the twelve signs on any angle, regardless of your Sun or other planetary placements.

The Twelve Houses

Houses are numbered from one to twelve, in a counterclockwise direction, beginning at the Ascendant and going down around the chart. A planet, therefore, has both a zodiacal position and a house position, and takes qualities from both the sign and house it is in. This shows how planetary energies become personalized and actually play themselves out in your life, or how you take the initiative to express them. Each pie-shaped wedge describes a number of potential physical and psychological manifestations, with considerable leeway for many possibilities.

Houses do not modify the planetary energies as signs do, but are spheres of activity, places where the energies appear in your life. A common analogy is to speak of planets as actors, signs as their roles, and houses as the stages on which they enact their parts. In other words, the planets are the *who* and *what,* the signs convey the *how,* and the houses are the *where.*

Just as with signs, there are ways of sorting houses. The most important groups fall into three categories: angular, succedent, and cadent houses, roughly analogous to cardinal, fixed and mutable signs.

Angular houses (1, 4, 7, 10) are considered to be the most powerful, because their energy is most easily expressed into the world in the four defining areas of human life: physical presence and appearance (1), home and family (4), relationships with others (especially marriage) (7), and career and public presence (10). This reflects the view that the angles, the primary structural framework of the horoscope, represent what most significantly characterizes and connects you with the greater world.

Succedent houses (2, 5, 8, 11) "succeed" or follow the angular houses and focus, in part, on money, resources and practical supports to accomplishments: what you own and earn (2), creative talents that translate into marketability (5), how you collaborate financially with others (8), and your personal and social networks (11).

Cadent houses (3, 6, 9, 12) were once thought to be less obvious, even weak. Modern astrology sees these placements as subtly significant, concerned with thinking processes (3), training and development of skills (6), belief systems (9), and mental and spiritual health that importantly support outer expression and success in life (12).

Modern astrologers' evaluation of cadent houses has been strongly modified by long-term research carried out by Michel and Françoise Gauquelin in both Europe and North America. Their painstaking statistical work with thousands of charts revealed that planetary placements in cadent houses, especially if close to angles, have an astonishing correlation to chosen careers and career success.

Here are generally agreed-upon meanings for the twelve houses:

First House/Ascendant: you and your image
The first house correlates to the spark of life and the resultant energy released into the world; physical birth and your physical body; your appearance, self-presentation, and mode of encountering the world; your projection of yourself into the environment.

Second House: values and gains from work

The second house refers to money (earned from a job) and portable possessions; your values, dictating how you attract and spend money; and the skills and talents that aid you in generating an income.

Third House: the near world; the "lower mind"

This sector encompasses the early learning environment and shaping of mental patterns, and, consequently, your everyday thinking; your style of communication in speaking and writing; early schooling, from pre-school through high school; your immediate environment or neighborhood, and relationships with people in them; your siblings and your relationships with them; and travel over short distances or for short periods of time.

Fourth House/IC: your inner foundation

The fourth house relates to the collective unconscious, the substratum of human consciousness linking us to the human race as a whole; the foundations of life that make you feel secure; ancestors and parents (perhaps especially the mother); home, property, real estate; and the final phase of life, or old age.

Fifth House: children, creativity, and personal pleasures

Besides children, this sector refers to creative efforts and products expressing your individuality; hobbies and pleasurable pastimes; recreation and amusements; dating and socializing not involving a deeper commitment; your romantic life; and gambling and risk-taking.

Sixth House: your labor or other people's labor

This area specifies work, the workplace, and working conditions—a job as opposed to a career; employees (fellow employees and your employees); service, servitude, and servants (in our time, service provided by cleaners, housekeepers, nannies, etc.); health and sickness (especially as physical health relates to emotional and mental health); aspects of hygiene, nutrition, diet, and lifestyle fostering healthy and efficient body functioning; and small animals or pets, likely because originally cats and dogs performed important functions on farms or in factories.

Seventh House/Descendant: others, marriage and partnership

Along with marriage or business partners (where legal agreements exist), this sector includes open (known) enemies; the type of relationships you attract, the way in which you relate to those closest to you, and the way you see them.

Eighth House: shared resources

The eighth house refers to money or property held in common with marriage or business partners (e.g., mutual funds, pooled money, real estate owned together); everything to do with finances and investments: discretionary money (left over after financial obligations are met) and its uses; negotiations with banks or other lending institutions; taxes and dealings with the government; wills and their contents (creation of trusts, etc.), and inheritances. It also includes death (the relinquishing of physical forms in the process of change) and the afterlife; psychological transformation through internal processing or external work with a therapist; the realm of the unknown or occult; and ritual work.

Ninth House: the faraway world, the "higher mind"

This sector describes education (after high school, both college/university and post-graduate); dissemination of knowledge through books and other forms of publishing; travel over long distances or for long periods of time, and goods bought and sold across international boundaries (i.e., importing and exporting); religion, philosophy, belief systems, metaphysics; and the law and legal matters.

Tenth House/Midheaven: your public life

The tenth house relates to your career, public role and social status, and reputation and prestige in society derived from these; and parent(s) (perhaps especially the father).

Eleventh House: friends and community associations

The eleventh house is a social one, encompassing friends as well as clubs, groups, and other social and community organizations you join; plans for your future; your hopes, wishes, and dreams; and possibly money earned as a result of career efforts, especially if you are self-employed.

Twelfth House: your hidden self

The mysterious twelfth house relates to the personal unconscious, what you may be unaware of in yourself that could be self-defeating; clandestine relationships and secret (unknown) enemies; places of withdrawal in order to heal (e.g., hospitals, asylums); places of isolation due to society's judgment of your faults or weaknesses (mental institutions, prisons, workhouses); places of withdrawal or retreat in order to cultivate experiences of connection to the greater whole or the divine (e.g., convents, monasteries); and large animals.

Notice that houses operate across the zodiac, as polarities. For instance, the second house is *your* money, while the eighth house, its opposite, is *other people's* money.

Houses can also be clustered together to reflect personal, social, and universal concerns. In houses 1 to 4, you ask "Who am I?" "What do I want and need?" "What do I think about things?" In houses 5 to 8, you question "How do I fit in to the working world?" "How do I create bonds with others?" "How do I make the most of what I have?" In houses 9 to 12, the issues are broader and more existential: "What do I believe?" "What is the role I am to play in this world?" "Where am I ultimately going?"

The Evolution of House Systems: A Historical Perspective

Today we have a number of house systems from which to choose, some of which are briefly discussed below. Among these are Equal House, Porphyry, Campanus, Regiomontanus, Placidus, and Morinus.

I recommend adopting one house system while you are learning, and experimenting with others later. I personally use Placidus, but switch to Equal House for births in more northerly latitudes. The Placidus house system is still the most popular worldwide; using it harmonizes your work with other astrologers.

What follows is a brief description of the historical development of some house systems. If you do not immediately comprehend this, do not be concerned. If it seems too technical, you can simply skim it or skip over it. An understanding of the astronomy and mathematics involved can be absorbed over time.

Since a horoscope attempts the impossible (capturing three-dimensional space on a two-dimensional piece of paper), no system is perfect. Each involves choices about how to divide the space between the Ascendant and the MC. For a clear and thorough explanation and evaluation of house systems, see *The Elements of House Division* by Ralph William Holden. For a comprehensive overall examination of the relevant astronomy, consult *The Astrologer's Astronomical Handbook* by Jeff Mayo.

Equal House: What began to bother astrologers using the Equal House system is that, while it divides space neatly into twelve equal parts like the segments of an orange, the Midheaven is not the same degree of the zodiac as the tenth house's starting point or "cusp." In fact, it may not be inside the tenth house at all. The Ascendant-Descendant and Midheaven-IC axes are rarely precisely ninety degrees from each other in the Equal House system.

Porphyry: As far as we know, in the third century c.e., Porphyry, writing in a commentary on Ptolemy's work, first suggested using the Ascendant, Descendant, Midheaven, and IC as the cusps of the first, seventh, tenth, and fourth houses. This was consistent with centuries of tradition stressing the importance of these major axes. He divided the degrees between these points equally to create the intermediate house cusps.

Astrology reached a low ebb in Europe during the next few centuries, now known as the Dark Ages. During this period, the center of intellectual activity shifted to the Middle East. Further attempts to address the disjunction between houses and angles were not made until the inauguration of the 12th-century Renaissance, when blended classical-Arabic knowledge (which included astrology) was reintroduced to Spain.

Campanus: The 12th-century Renaissance, which disseminated mathematical and trigonometric knowledge from Arabic sources as a result of the Muslim conquest of Spain, stimulated further exploration of different astrological house systems. Johannes *Campanus*, an accomplished mathematician and Chaplain to Pope Urban IV in the 13th century, built on Porphyry's use of the Midheaven and IC as cusps of the tenth and fourth houses, but changed the reference point for calculation of the intermediate house cusps to the prime vertical, creating a space-based system.

The prime vertical is the vertical circle that passes through the zenith and nadir (points directly overhead and underneath the observer at a particular place on the Earth's surface) **and** the east and west points of the horizon. Campanus wanted to create houses of equal volume, all related strictly to the Earth's daily rotation and not to the Sun's movement along the ecliptic. So Campanus houses trisect each of the quadrants of the prime vertical. With this change, the door was truly opened to tinkering with Ptolemaic tradition.

Regiomontanus: In the 15th century, a professor of astronomy in Vienna named Johannes Muller, but better known as *Regiomontanus,* took Campanus' work one step further. A translator of Ptolemy's *Almagest*, Regiomontanus published books on mathematics and some of the earliest printed ephemerides. He suggested that house construction be made completely consistent with Earth's daily rotation. To do this, he used the celestial equator (and not the prime vertical) as the reference point for creating house cusps, by trisecting the quadrants of the celestial equator.

Morinus: A doctor of medicine and professor of mathematics at the University of Paris in the 17th century, Morinus was so respected as an astrologer that he was retained by the powerful Cardinal Richelieu. Morinus followed Regiomontanus in using the celestial equator as the great circle on which to base twelve equal houses. Abandoning any reference at all to the ecliptic, Morinus' houses have the advantage of not varying with latitude. However, since neither the MC nor Ascendant is a house cusp and the system does not reference the ecliptic at all, Morinus' system has few followers.

Placidus: Later in the 17th century, a monk and professor of mathematics at the University of Padua named *Placidus* de Tito proposed discarding previous methods of house creation and substituting a method derived from the motion of the rising degree through the ecliptic during the full 24-hour day (a time-based system). This may go back to a much earlier method proposed by the Arabic astrologer Alchabitus in the 12th century.

The elaboration did not stop there. In the centuries following, other approaches were put forward, some just variations on ones already proposed. All of these fall into three categories: ecliptic-based, space-based, or timed-based methods. Debate about which system to use has carried into our times, with Placidus' method popular in North America because central figures in the revival of astrology in the 19th century used tables of Placidus houses.

All of these discoveries have produced a dilemma for modern students of astrology. With so many house systems or variants to consider, which should you use? Ideally, that decision should be based on some understanding of mathematics and astronomy, but many students of astrology adopt their teacher's house system without grasping why they are using it. Some systems are thought to be especially suited to certain subdivisions of astrology: Placidus for psychological analysis, for example.

Many of the house systems create more and more distorted charts the farther north you go on the planet, creating some houses bizarrely small and others huge. For that reason, astrologers living or working in the far north or casting charts for people born in northerly latitudes like England and Scandinavia tend to retain the Equal House system.

Ebertin: With so much difference of opinion and practice, why use houses at all? The Ebertin school of astrology, developed in Germany in the 20th century, dispensed with houses altogether, preferring to focus on planets in the signs, aspects between planets, angles of the chart, and midpoint combinations of two or more planetary factors. But what is lost with this method is the principal reason for using houses: seeing how the more universal energies of the planets, colored by their sign placements, actually manifest in specific ways in our lives.

I recommend you examine your own chart, as well as charts of famous people, to see how interpretations using other house systems match what you know of yourself and what you observe in others' public lives. Different house systems may place some planets in different houses, altering their possible expression in your life. Bear in mind, though, that some astrologers consider a planet within a few degrees of the next house cusp to have some influence in that area as well.

Computers now make it possible to calculate your own horoscope in every known house system in a matter of minutes—a task that would have taken many tedious days before the 1980s. After experimenting, you can decide which system is most insightful for you.

Each house system is a chosen lens on reality, and each can contribute insights into the soul's appearance in time. All house systems are ultimately imperfect efforts to squeeze the greater into the lesser. That implies that no single house system gives you the full story; each gives a partial picture of the mystery of incarnation.

Interception

All house systems (except Equal House, of course) generate charts with different-sized houses, some greater and some smaller. Bigger houses may indicate areas of life that have greater importance and relevance to you. Some house systems create house divisions so large (more than thirty degrees) that a single house can contain an entire sign—i.e., one whose boundaries do not touch either that house's cusp or the next one. This phenomenon is called "interception." Such an extra-large house actually contains three signs: the sign on the cusp of that house, the intercepted sign contained within it, and the beginning of the next sign that is also on the cusp of the next house. In that case, all three signs play a part in the affairs of that house, creating complexity of interpretation. (To see an example of an intercepted sign, look ahead to Oprah Winfrey's chart in Part II. Notice that the sign Capricorn is contained within the first house, and that the sign Cancer is wholly contained within the seventh house.)

Astrologers generally believe that the qualities of the intercepted sign are more difficult to access. If there are planets in that sign, they may express themselves only after significant activation or later in life. You may also have to work harder to extract their potentials, and rely on yourself rather than others to accomplish your success.

Planets in the Twelve Houses

The astrological tradition about houses provides an important way of focusing planetary energies into differentiated spheres of life, and making more precise determinations about individual psychology and potential events. Now we can blend the meanings associated with each planet with its house placement, the next step in a more integrated interpretation.

The Sun in the Houses

One of the most important placements in the horoscope is the Sun's house position, which can highlight one's main life purpose. The Sun may express itself as follows:

Sun in the First House: a strong need to focus on yourself and your own development and then to express your personality confidently to the world. This position can foster a forceful drive to project yourself into the environment so that others experience you as a strong and dominant presence.

Watch for: attention getting; relating everything to yourself; overwhelming others.

Sun in the Second House: a motivation to use your skills and talents to generate income and attract possessions that create long-term material and psychological security. Clarifying values and attitudes can motivate you to develop abilities that increase your desirability in the marketplace, and so increase your salary.

Watch for: over-attachment to tangible assets (like Charles Dickens' Scrooge) leading to greed or hoarding that narrows your life focus.

Sun in the Third House: a need to develop the everyday mind so that through reading, study, or absorbing information about daily events, you can communicate easily with others in the immediate environment. You may be a "connector," providing information to others (as a teacher) or literally transporting goods (as a messenger).

Watch for: overvaluing information that has only temporary use (fads and fancies); fixating on continually adapting to changing circumstances so that the nervous system is constantly stressed.

Sun in the Fourth House: a need to establish an emotionally secure foundation in life, either through clearing up early childhood or parental issues on a psychological level or probing the deeper collective unconscious through working with images. Establishing a physical home and putting down roots is deeply fulfilling.

Watch for: over-attachment to family, tribe, or physical home to the point where you are afraid to leave it or cannot see others' perspectives; being held back by the past.

Sun in the Fifth House: a drive to express yourself confidently and spontaneously through creation and/or procreation, beginning with experiencing the joy of play in childhood and leading to an ability to take pleasure in hobbies and games later in life, especially the game of love and romance.

Watch for: treating life as a game so you take nothing seriously and are unable to make adult commitments; being undependable; continually seeking an audience to applaud your creative efforts.

Sun in the Sixth House: a desire to integrate yourself usefully into the workplace (in other words, find a job), to serve practically and efficiently. There is also a need to monitor your body so that all its organs and functions collaborate to create optimum health, supporting your ability to go to work every day.

Watch for: being a workaholic; having your innately self-sacrificing nature exploited; putting yourself under pressure to perform perfectly or have perfect health; being a hypochondriac.

Sun in the Seventh House: a need to link yourself with another in marriage or partnership to feel fulfilled. There is a need to form bonds that complement you and express a healthy balance between what Martin Buber described as "I" and "Thou."

Watch for: over-dependency on a partner; immersion in a relationship to the point of diminishing yourself; getting into inappropriate relationships through insecurity or fear of being alone.

Sun in the Eighth House: collaboration with others to maximize investments, and then developing within yourself a talent for accumulating wealth and gaining influence. This empowerment can be facilitated by exploring psychological states to release energy and regenerate yourself or others, or probing numinous or taboo areas of life (sex, magic, birth, and death) to release energy.

Watch for: manipulation or exploitation of others (or by others of you); accruing wealth at others' expense; repressing emotion leading to warped psychological states or odd behavior.

Sun in the Ninth House: a need to broaden your understanding through education or travel, or expand into a wider global or historical environment in order to discover life's deepest meaning. This may involve study of religious or philosophical traditions, working with foreigners or living in foreign countries, or passing on established traditions that encapsulate the wisdom of centuries.

Watch for: being superficial due to lack of disciplined study; thinking your truth is good for everybody; adhering to dogma formulated by others due to your laziness or insecurity.

Sun in the Tenth House: a desire to be a success (however you define that) in the eyes of the world. Usually "success" means being a recognized leader or authority in your field, and gaining the prestige or "perks" that come from reaching the top. Achievements are secured by determining goals, being ambitious, and working hard to attain a social position.

Watch for: over-focus on career to the detriment of personal or family life with a resultant unemotional one-sidedness; being bound by your role or your ego; being authoritarian or corrupted by having influence or rank.

Sun in the Eleventh House: joining with friends, groups, or community organizations that allow self-expression and yet satisfy your need to connect and cooperate with others to accomplish altruistic goals of improving life for some segment of society. The need here is to make an impact on the community or culture, possibly through your vision of a better future.
Watch for: over-identification with the group; neglecting one-on-one intimacy; being overly influenced by friends' ideals or opinions.

Sun in the Twelfth House: a demand to cultivate a rewarding inner life in practicing meditation and following spiritual paths that connect you to the divine through mystical and transcendant experiences. Periods of withdrawal catalyze this, during which you may be challenged to confront humanity's essential aloneness. You may also need to be of spiritual service (perhaps as a counselor or person who prays for others, or who directs healing energy to others) in subtle, unobtrusive ways.
Watch for: over-isolating yourself; feeling limited or victimized by fate or your own hidden weaknesses; escapism through drugs or alcohol.

The Moon in the Houses

The Moon's house placement shows the emotional focus of the chart, the place where you hope to find emotional satisfaction and security. This can highlight areas you feel most deeply about and also where you have the greatest emotional need. Here, you are most sensitive and receptive, as well as emotionally expressive. The Moon may express itself as follows:

Moon in the First House: heightened sensitivity to the environment, especially others' energetic expression and feeling states. Your emotional responses to places and people can be strong, but very changeable. You can easily project protective and maternal feelings to others around you.
Watch for: over-impressionability or being too easily influenced by others; moodiness; being easily distracted.

Moon in the Second House: an especially strong need to examine values and find security through money and material possessions.

Emotions can influence your ability to earn money, and your financial situation can fluctuate. Attitudes to money can evolve over time. *Watch for:* excessive attachment to money and personal possessions; substituting them for personal relationships.

Moon in the Third House: thoughts are highly influenced by feelings so that they change rapidly, leading to an ability to free-associate, or to a talent for poetic or descriptive speaking or writing. As a result, you can be verbally fluent and very talkative in a stream-of-consciousness way. You may enjoy talking about feelings, and may be a good mimic of others' bodies and voices.
Watch for: intellectualizing emotions; being unclear about ideas or having superficial opinions due to their changeability.

Moon in the Fourth House: a strong emotional attachment to mother, family, home, and roots. The need to secure roots and establish a home base can be frustrated by a continually evolving internal picture of the ideal home, and so the physical home can be difficult to stabilize or constantly change. You may have a natural attunement to an inner world of images, and so be mediumistic.
Watch for: dependency on an external home to provide an emotional anchor instead of developing solid inner security; unhealthy enmeshment with family.

Moon in the Fifth House: emotions are the spur to your creativity. You may want children very much, though there may be issues around fertility. You may easily connect emotionally to children, whether your own or others' (which can make you a born teacher or caretaker of young children). Romantic involvements are attractive, but extremely changeable.
Watch for: taking excessive risks in gambling with life or love affairs; being disinclined to make commitments and fickle in romance.

Moon in the Sixth House: emotional attachments to the workplace and your fellow employees. You may be especially capable of giving caring service to the public. You may need variety at work, and adapt easily to changing work conditions. Emotions strongly influence health.
Watch for: investing work with emotional energy that should also find outlets in family and relationship life; being unable to stick to a job; having emotional stress create real or psychosomatic conditions.

Moon in the Seventh House: strong emotional need for and involvement with a partner, starting even when you are very young. You may attract a partner who is sensitive and deeply feeling, and you can adjust quickly to your partner's emotional states. You may also be maternal or childlike in a relationship.

Watch for: over-adapting to your partner; staying in a relationship for security reasons; wanting a relationship, but being unable to respond deeply emotionally.

Moon in the Eighth House: an instinctive awareness of others' inner feelings or secrets that may make you an effective therapist or counselor. You may have powerful emotional and sexual drives, and these strongly influence your psychological (or even physical) health. Strong intuitions may influence investment decisions.

Watch for: repressed feelings creating emotional or mental blocks or distortions in attitudes or behaviors; confusion in making clear decisions about finances; ability to tune into others, tempting one to take advantage of them.

Moon in the Ninth House: strong emotional attachments to foreign places and people. An emotional need for freedom can express itself through a love of travel and adventures. Emotional security comes from identification with a religious belief system or educational institution. You may especially enjoy studying and learning.

Watch for: restlessness that prevents you from settling anywhere or making up your mind about your beliefs; having a superficial approach to deeper truths.

Moon in the Tenth House: great satisfaction from emotional commitment to a career and from career achievements. Your career may be of a caretaking type, where you can express nurturance and caring. It may go through changes, as you go in and out of favor with bosses or authority figures. You may have a special talent for sensing the "public pulse," so you may be good at spotting trends.

Watch for: vacillating or being uncertain about your career; losing touch with your personal life and genuine feelings due to over-identification with your public role.

Moon in the Eleventh House: strong attachment to friends or communal groups. You likely enjoy socializing with a constantly changing group of associates, and you can adapt easily to new people. You may have a special interest in helping women and children.

Watch for: being unable to stay focused on goals or committed to projects, or sustain involvements with groups over time; being friendly but only superficially connected to friends.

Moon in the Twelfth House: a deep need for seclusion in order to recharge emotional batteries and recover psychic balance due to resonance to people and places. You may be able to tune into others' emotional states psychically, and thus be a good spiritual counselor. Emotional satisfaction may come from spiritual experiences or compassionate service for the highest and greatest good.
Watch for: being confused about your own feelings due to emotional interference from others; having difficulty getting in touch with your own feelings and erroneously thinking you have transcended feelings altogether.

Mercury in the Houses

Mercury's house placement shows the intellectual focus of the chart: where your thinking may be focused and where your intellectual energy may be directed. It may also color the way your mind works. Mercury may express itself as follows:

Mercury in the First House: a strongly rational way of interacting with the immediate environment. You may be a high-strung person with an active nervous system, quick to respond to changes around you and clever and fluent in self-presentation.
Watch for: being restless and constantly on the go, with a tendency to be talkative or perhaps have nervous habits or tics.

Mercury in the Second House: thoughts focused on determining values and accruing money and other possessions. You may use mental talents to earn a living and may be clever and resourceful in finding ways to increase your income.
Watch for: taking short cuts or using questionable tactics to make gains; talking and thinking about material things while missing their real value or use.

Mercury in the Third House: increased mental activity, with a busy and highly curious mind. You may be articulate and capable of quick or witty repartee, or take delight in dialogue or debate, and so be attracted to professions related to sales, teaching, or travel.
Watch for: being superficial or a dilettante about study or education; arriving at ideas without careful thought; valuing fluency over con-

tent; delighting in intellectual superiority or overwhelming others with a constant stream of verbiage.

Mercury in the Fourth House: strong intellectual interests in the past, family history, and geneology. You may have a good library in your home or enjoy mental or physical comings and goings from home base. Emotions may color thought processes. One gift of this placement may be a good memory.

Watch for: being stuck in conventional or old-fashioned thinking if thought patterns are too influenced by parents or the past, since ideas transmitted by earlier generations may be outdated; frequent changes of residence.

Mercury in the Fifth House: mental and verbal creativity expressed in dramatic and spontaneous ways, like improvization or story-telling. You may love intellectual fun and games (practical jokes, crossword puzzles, sudoku, bridge), and be a gifted mimic of others' words or actions.

Watch for: wanting to show off your intellectual knowledge or creative ideas; being a good seducer or con artist; being naïve in thinking.

Mercury in the Sixth House: lively comunication in the workplace, possibly through contributing helpful and practical suggestions for greater productivity or efficiency. You may have a flexible, analytical mind gifted in making intelligent decisions and capable of handling details.

Watch for: over-stimulation of the brain and nervous system creating health problems, particularly in an uncongenial work environment; tendencies to worry or be a perfectionist, which could make you dissatisfied with yourself and your work.

Mercury in the Seventh House: a need for mental rapport with partners and ongoing communication in important relationships. You may be attracted to a bright or witty partner or someone who is constantly changing. You may have a natural ability to connect with others, and a great curiosity about relationship dynamics.

Watch for: being unreliable in commitments or attracting a partner who is hard to pin down; being reluctant to reveal your true opinions, either because you are overly adaptable or overly influenced by your partner's ideas.

Mercury in the Eighth House: active discussion of profound or complex topics like finances and investments, psychological strategies, or esoteric and occult studies. The mind is deepened and capable of in-depth probing and research (which could make you a talented detective, spy, or gossip columnist). Your words may have a persuasive power (as in advertising, propaganda, rituals, or magic), and you can forcefully influence others.
Watch for: not telling what you know, but enjoying getting others to reveal their thoughts and secrets; using your knowledge or mental powers to manipulate and take advantage of others; plotting and scheming.

Mercury in the Ninth House: great curiosity and mental interest in religion, philosophy, metaphysics, education, and foreign languages and cultures. You may be driven to learn constantly and love to travel to engage new experiences. You may enjoy making profound truths comprehensible and accessible to people.
Watch for: over-simplifying or trivializing deeper truths through laziness or the opportunity to "sell" them; restlessness preventing you from staying long enough in one place to enjoy it; being content with a superficial understanding of a weighty topic.

Mercury in the Tenth House: choice of an occupation that demands good speaking or writing skills. You may need a career that offers variety and intellectual challenges, with opportunities to develop your skills and talents.
Watch for: continual changes in jobs or career because of boredom; relying on superficial brilliance to make a positive impression in your profession.

Mercury in the Eleventh House: enjoying lively dialogues with friends who share similar intellectual interests. You may be sociable and make friends easily, possessing the ability to talk comfortably with anyone.
Watch for: using friendships to your advantage; having intellectual exchange dominate over emotional connectedness; changing friends frequently.

Mercury in the Twelfth House: thinking may be colored by the unconscious, leading to intuitive thinking or easier communication through images, symbols, and metaphors. You may have strong intellectual interests in spirituality, mysticism, or art. You can use the mind as a springboard to spiritual experience (as in raja yoga).

Watch for: unclear or unrealistic thinking; being disinclined to talk at all (though you can be articulate when dealing with people in need or in crisis).

Venus in the Houses

The house position of Venus reveals areas of life that you especially enjoy and take pleasure in exploring. Here you may have artistic talent that can be used to generate wealth. The house placement also shows how and where you attract others, make friends, and find possible partners. Venus may express itself as follows:

Venus in the First House: an enhanced ability to project a charming and friendly personality that easily draws and impresses others. You may have a particularly alluring appearance and be fashionable and well groomed. The gift of "likability" may make you popular.
Watch for: using an awareness of your effect on others to advantage; being lazy and vain; relying on superficial appearance and not developing depth of character.

Venus in the Second House: a strong love of money and material things, which you may easily attract to enhance feelings of security. You may earn money through the arts, since you may have good taste and an instinct for an item's true value.
Watch for: overspending on luxuries (art, jewelry, clothing); being too focused on gratifying material and sensual needs; expecting that "money can buy love."

Venus in the Third House: the gift of "charming speech," giving thoughts and words a graceful expression so you can easily persuade or entertain others. You may be able to use language diplomatically to soften disagreements. Communication may be fluent, and you may love playing with language.
Watch for: using words to flatter or seduce; playing mental games; being shallow or insincere in speech.

Venus in the Fourth House: a great love of home, family, and roots. You need a pleasant home that has a friendly and harmonious atmosphere where you can express yourself artistically. Family members may be your best friends.
Watch for: being too attached to parents, to the ancestral home, or the area in which you live; needing "peace at any price" at home.

Venus in the Fifth House: great energy for socializing and romance, drawing partners easily by making a good impression through an attractive appearance. A high level of artistic talent and creativity is likely. You may take great pleasure from having children, or having warm and comfortable relationships with children in general.
Watch for: being the flirt who is superficial in love; loving to be "in love with love."

Venus in the Sixth House: loving your work (and possibly even finding love in the workplace) and being successful at work due to your charm, friendliness, and cooperative attitude. You may bring an artistic flair to the work situation, or work in a field related to the arts.
Watch for: socializing that distracts from accomplishing work goals; having health affected by a disharmonious working environment.

Venus in the Seventh House: an especially happy partnership or marriage. You may draw very attractive people to you or prefer to connect with those who are friendly and fashionable. You likely have considerable social skills that harmonize you with another or others.
Watch for: depending on others for approval; wanting relationships to be easy and not having to work on them; taking advantage of a partner for material benefits.

Venus in the Eighth House: a need for intense relationships with emotional depth and sexual passion. You may enjoy using your abilities, contacts, and resources to increase wealth, so that your financial situation increases steadily over time from good advice, "hot tips," or inheritances. Art may be used to explore forbidden areas, and you may be attracted to the taboo and perverse.
Watch for: being seductive, calculating, and manipulative in order to make gains; seeing love as a business; exploiting the power you have over a partner.

Venus in the Ninth House: a love of learning or religious studies, being especially responsive to encouraging teachers or beautiful art in places of worship. Love and compassion may be your essential religious values. You may enjoy traveling to pleasant places where you can make friends, find business opportunities, or even a marriage partner.
Watch for: socializing at your place of worship instead of seeking deeper truths; being lazy about studies or explorations and so adopting others' ideas or dogmas as your own; being a dilettante.

Venus in the Tenth House: a love of work and appreciation of pleasant and presentable associates. You may have a creative flair in your career, or pursue a career in the arts, or be motivated to bring beauty into the world. Sociability and popularity can positively impress others, bestowing a fine reputation and financial gain.
Watch for: using your charm in a calculating way to get ahead; oversocializing in the workplace; losing authority by making everyone you work with a friend.

Venus in the Eleventh House: an outstanding ability to make and keep many friends, and taking great pleasure in being in social groups to which you can bring a special harmony and grace. You may be drawn to community organizations with artistic or cultural leanings, or associations that seek to put compassion into action.
Watch for: being a pleaser or flatterer in order to retain friendships; spreading yourself thin in many superficial friendships or group affiliations.

Venus in the Twelfth House: aspiring to offer compassionate or charitable service unselfishly through love of the divine (as in bhakti yoga). You may cultivate artistic inspiration by attuning to a transcendent dimension where creative ideas originate and entities like the ancient Greek Muses are thought to exist. You may desire a soul-based love, or identify your partner as the Divine Beloved so that your relationship has a spiritual dimension.
Watch for: keeping relationships secret or engaging in clandestine involvements; substituting a fantasy love for real engagement with a human partner; being disinclined to socialize.

Mars in the Houses

Mars' house placement targets areas in your life where your personal energy finds an outlet, where you assert yourself, or may even be aggressive. Here there is abundant energy for action. Here you may take a stand or fight on behalf of the affairs of that house. Mars may express itself as follows:

Mars in the First House: a strongly assertive and forthright personality with masculine overtones. You easily go after what you want. You may have potential to be a leader, with a warrior-like fearlessness and determination.

Watch for: intimidating and dominating others; always putting your own demands first; constantly getting into trouble through impulsive actions.

Mars in the Second House: energetic pursuit of what you want materially. You may work consistently over a long time to establish material security. Money may come through active physical work.
Watch for: having as much energy for spending as for earning; fighting over resources; gambling or taking other impulsive financial risks.

Mars in the Third House: constant mental activity leading to quick responses in mind and body, with fast reflexes and manual dexterity. You may courageously defend your ideas by challenging others to debate and can speak authoritatively and commandingly. You may make a good critic, satirist, or sarcastic wit.
Watch for: nervous exhaustion; being argumentative and tactless; restless energy leading to compulsive movements or short jaunts.

Mars in the Fourth House: being busy in the home, using much energy to clean, renovate, exercise in a home gym, or pursue home-improvement projects. There is great energy for competitive activities like sports with the family. You are capable of staunchly defending home territory.
Watch for: dominating the home environment; suppressing anger at family members, so that you seethe instead of engage in honest confrontation or move out.

Mars in the Fifth House: active engagement in romantic conquests, and being highly sensual and sexual in romantic affairs. You may enthusiastically enjoy life, excel at competitive games and sports, and eagerly participate in creative activities.
Watch for: conflict or upsets in affairs of the heart; losses through gambling in love and life; creative efforts turning others off by displays of ego.

Mars in the Sixth House: being hardworking, decisive, and ambitious on the job, where you may be stimulated by a friendly spirit of rivalry with coworkers. You are impelled to be the best or do the best job possible. You can take action in order to sustain or improve good health.

Watch for: inconsideration or lack of cooperation leading to conflict with coworkers or bosses; being impatient with or tyrannizing subordinates; letting unresolved anger affect health.

Mars in the Seventh House: investing yourself energetically in relationships or partnerships. You may be active socially or physically with others, as in competitions or sports. You may be assertive with your partner or gravitate to strong personalities.
Watch for: struggling for dominance in a relationship instead of finding a workable balance; offending others through aggressive stances or lack of adaptability.

Mars in the Eighth House: exerting tremendous energy to accumulate resources through investments involving you in business and finance. You may be highy sexed and want to explore all aspects of sexuality or use sexual energy for transformation, as in tantric practices. You may investigate magic or the occult, or probe the mysteries of life and death.
Watch for: taking dangerous personal and financial risks; allowing personal resentments to tempt you to undermine or manipulate others.

Mars in the Ninth House: fervent religious feelings and passionate attachments to religions, philosophies, and ideals that you can courageously and forcefully defend. There is much mental activity, and you may be passionate about learning, especially related to foreign or bygone languages and cultures. A restless need for exploration leads to travel and adventures in distant places.
Watch for: offending others by challenging their belief systems; being a fanatic, intolerant know-it-all; browbeating others by threatening them with punishment by an avenging God.

Mars in the Tenth House: enormous energy exerted to climb the professional ladder and establish a social position. Ambition and a drive for success may impel you to operate autonomously within a division of a company or to be independently self-employed.
Watch for: making enemies by being overly competitive, power hungry, or overbearing with professional colleagues; disregarding the rules because you think you are above them.

Mars in the Eleventh House: being active with many friends, for whom you can strongly advocate. You may be passionate about helping to correct social injustices through cooperative ventures that may be political or sports-related. A natural crusader, you may spearhead group efforts to improve the community.

Watch for: conflict with friends due to your inability to agree with group goals; insisting that your personal goals be adopted by others; squandering energy in excessive socializing or organizational commitments.

Mars in the Twelfth House: by dedicating personal energy to higher purposes or using personal energy in spiritually infused activities like martial arts. You may be successful through working behind the scenes, and can be a gifted strategist. You may champion the underdog or defend the defenseless.

Watch for: suppressing energy so that you cannot advocate for yourself due to fear of repercussions or retaliation; bottling up anger; repressing sexuality; engaging in self-defeating behavior so that you are your own worst enemy.

Jupiter in the Houses

Jupiter's house placement points to potential areas of growth and expansion, and areas where you may gain wisdom during your life. You may be lucky here, especially materially. This may be due to a positive and optimistic attitude that encourages situations to resolve in your favor. Religious or philosophical principles find outlets here. The house position can also pinpoint areas where you may be lazy or overconfident. Jupiter expresses itself as follows:

Jupiter in the First House: a cheerful and outgoing energy, creating a positive impression on others, who are disposed to aid you. With a naturally happy temperament and an enthusiasm for life, you can make others around you feel better. You can present a wealthy and benevolent appearance. Buoyant energy protects health.

Watch for: assuming everything will go your way without much effort; being self-indulgent and lazy; feeling entitled or "lording it" over others.

Jupiter in the Second House: wealth and prosperity, or at least the feeling that you are richly blessed. You may also be generous and share your good fortune with others. Having a philanthropic nature motivates you to use your wealth to improve others' lives because you trust that your income will continue to flow.

Watch for: spending beyond your means; taking financial risks due to foolish overconfidence; expecting to be paid despite a disinclination to work.

Jupiter in the Third House: expanding your everyday mind to try and grasp broader concepts and a larger vision. You may be able to learn easily or have supportive teachers so that you benefit from education. You may also have positive experiences with siblings, relatives, or neighbors.

Watch for: having a restless and overactive mind, talking excessively and not listening to others; being unable to translate grand ideas into workable solutions; presuming that your opinions are always right.

Jupiter in the Fourth House: luck or good fortune through the status or wealth of parents who can provide a large and comfortable childhood home along with other benefits. Later, you may desire a spacious and elegantly decorated home yourself. You may have luck with real estate, even owning more than one property.

Watch for: feeling superior due to family reputation or wealth; moving often due to feeling restless and dissatisfied with home.

Jupiter in the Fifth House: an exuberant love of romantic adventures that may teach you much. This placement brings a confident and inexhaustible creativity as well as luck in taking chances. You may benefit from children, with whom you have a warm and affectionate relationship.

Watch for: dissipating energy as a Don Juan or "Donna Juanette"; excessive gambling or risk-taking; spreading yourself too thin in fun activities.

Jupiter in the Sixth House: a positive attitude in the workplace that uplifts coworkers and enlists their cooperation. You enjoy a comfortable and spacious working environment where you may be liberally rewarded materially. This position also protects health.

Watch for: over-indulgence in food and drink that brings health problems, especially with the liver; being overly sociable or gregarious on the job, encouraging inefficiency; ignoring details or skipping the harder aspects of your job.

Jupiter in the Seventh House: attracting wealthy or influential partners who may be good-natured and generous. You can gain materially through associations with others. Your natural friendliness can bring many associations.

Watch for: expecting your partner to give you status or take care of you without your reciprocating; expecting relationships to be easy and so neglecting your responsibilities.

Jupiter in the Eighth House: savvy in creating wealth from fortunate investments because of "hot tips" or your own intuition. Benefits come through others, through gifts or inheritances. You can over-come psychological difficulties or be helpful and supportive to others in crisis. You may seek wisdom through esoteric knowledge.
Watch for: excessive sexual involvements; financial risk-taking due to overconfidence leading to losses.

Jupiter in the Ninth House: a naturally philosophical and religious temperament, with great faith in a beneficent Universe. A broad and tolerant vision makes you a wise counselor or religious advisor. Both education and travel can be enjoyable, as they provide experiences through which you gain insights.
Watch for: exaggerated or extreme views; arrogant presumption of the superiority of your views; restlessness leading to constant travel; being the eternal student who never graduates.

Jupiter in the Tenth House: success in career through abundant opportunities, and through gaining the respect of others through wise and benevolent leadership. You may be a visionary who pro-motes tolerance and understanding, and inspires others.
Watch for: having an exaggerated belief in your abilities or your role in the world; expecting attainment to be easy and so disdaining hard work; presuming others will sponsor, mentor, or follow you once you have achieved status.

Jupiter in the Eleventh House: a sociable and gregarious nature enjoying a wide circle of friends. You may share a philosophical or religious vision with friends or fellow group members who cooperate with you to improve some aspect of society. Friends can be especially generous or emotionally and materially supportive.
Watch for: wasting time and energy in the social scene; being fool-ishly confident about the future and doing nothing practical to realize your goals; misconstruing acquaintances as friends.

Jupiter in the Twelfth House: great faith in the spiritual dimension; in fact, you seem to have a guardian angel protecting you from the worst. You may be drawn to spiritual or mystical teachings and benefit from faithful pursuit of a spiritual path that releases your innate wisdom.

Watch for: withdrawing from the world because of disappointments or dissatisfaction; disdaining wealth or material possessions in favor of immaterial truth; expecting spiritual progress to be easy.

Saturn in the Houses

Saturn's placement in the horoscope shows where you initially meet limitations and obstacles, and struggle to grow. In the affairs of that house you learn some of the most important lessons in your life. Because of Saturn's essence as the "great teacher," no "Watch for" cautions are included here. Though Saturn is slow to release its potential, if you are committed, realistic, and hardworking in the related areas and face your fears, you will create solid success. Saturn may express itself as follows:

Saturn in the First House: overbearing parental, religious, or social restrictions that cause you to lose confidence so that you may be shy in self-expression and timid in self-assertion. By developing disciplined self-reliance, you may become more relaxed and comfortable in dealing with the world. If Saturn is close to the Ascendant, it can indicate a difficult birth.

Saturn in the Second House: fear of poverty or lack of material security. You may be timid about investing and miss financial opportunities or undervalue your skills and talents and so work for less than you deserve. By cultivating an inner feeling of self-worth, and investing in items of genuine value, you can prudently and responsibly build material wealth.

Saturn in the Third House: overcoming a lack of confidence in your mental abilities and verbal expression by slowing down the mind, weighing your words, and applying yourself steadily to your studies. In extreme cases, there may be learning difficulties or impediments in speech, like stuttering, or you may simply be a "reluctant reader." Being mentally disciplined and concentrating on a few key concepts or important areas of study, you can become an expert writer and speaker whose words carry weight.

Saturn in the Fourth House: inhibited by early childhood traumas, limited family circumstances, or an overbearing or fearsome parent so that you may need to overcome emotional negativity in the home. You may initially live in limited circumstances (basement apartments or small rooms), but gradually build up inner trust with strong foundations, reflected outwardly as a securely established home or solid investments in real estate.

Saturn in the Fifth House: a serious attitude toward romance, and either avoiding dating or trying to secure a relationship too soon. A lack of confidence in creativity can be overcome by studying the practical aspects of a creative field and patiently rehearsing until you gain confidence for performance. You may assume responsibilities for children and take parental duties seriously, or be a good teacher. You may not have children of your own, or only one to whom you are devoted.

Saturn in the Sixth House: too willing to take on routine work or drudgery in uncongenial workplaces. A patient acceptance of the necessity of hard work and careful looking after details may eventually lead to a Zen-like appreciation of even the smallest part of the job. You may have health problems (some resulting from worry), especially with bones and teeth, but you may actually have a strong constitution, helped by a disciplined approach to diet and lifestyle.

Saturn in the Seventh House: initial disappointments in partnerships or marriage, possibly due to reluctance to reveal yourself because of fear of hurt or rejection. You may marry for security or stay in a relationship for the sake of the outward form. You may marry late, or marry someone older or very emotionally mature, and then discover that you can be a responsible, faithful, and caring partner in an enduring relationship.

Saturn in the Eighth House: challenges regarding mutually shared investments, perhaps in disagreements about how to allot monies or in losses through poor judgment. You can be serious about sexual relations or experience blocked sexual expression due to fear of losing control or of deep intimacy. Developing inner emotional security and confidence in your intuition can eventually enable you to look after others' wealth (as well as your own) reliably to make steady financial gains.

Saturn in the Ninth House: delaying or preventing educational and travel opportunities, sometimes making travel onerous or only possible for serious purposes like work or study. You may be beset by religious doubts or fears, especially if you believe in a harsh or unforgiving God. You may need to rethink the religious or philosophical beliefs you were taught when young, especially if they were conservative and traditional, and painstakingly construct your own. Sustained mental effort over time or later in life can ultimately stabilize and concentrate your mind and lead to recognized intellectual accomplishments.

Saturn in the Tenth House: a lack of confidence to take a role in public life through fears of failure or feelings of inadequacy. You may undermine your own success, and so have to start a career all over again—the typical "fall from grace" pattern associated with this position. Being stable, responsible, and hardworking over time can build a solid reputation. Success comes at last as you develop expertise and are seen as a true professional and master within your field.

Saturn in the Eleventh House: initial mistrust of friends or shunning membership in groups or social activities because of shyness and insecurity. You may initially feel friendless, but eventually cultivate a few close friends who are dependable and life-long. They may be older or well-established and share your serious commitment to improving some aspect of community life. You can make visionary ideas practical by concentrating your efforts in areas where real change is possible.

Saturn in the Twelfth House: deep-seated fears of isolation, especially if imposed and not self-chosen. You may need to go into seclusion yourself or work with those confined in order to overcome subconscious blocks and unearth your innate wisdom. Learning to trust the Universe, having faith in a divine order, and faithfully practicing disciplines connecting you to something greater may enable you to offer true spiritual service in a spirit of devotion and humility.

The Outer Planets in the Houses

Uranus, Neptune, and Pluto carry meanings that relate to the collective, or to such high-frequency potentials that they often correlate with long-term cycles for large groups, nations, or even the world. Their house placements in an individual's horoscope allow these transpersonal factors to be experienced personally. Because of the obvious challenges inherent in handling these unusual energies, no "Watch for" cautions are mentioned in the following sections.

Uranus in the Houses

The placement of Uranus by house indicates where you are the most creative, inventive, and unconventional. In these areas, you seek the greatest freedom of thought and action, so you may appear erratic or changeable. Here you experience circumstances beyond your control. It is a locus of genius—or cosmic chaos. Uranus may express itself as follows:

Uranus in the First House: an unconventional appearance or unique personality that either radiates a nervous energy or an electric charisma. The strong need for personal freedom may make you appear rebellious and restless, willful and impatient. You may feel different or special or alienated from your surroundings, but you can be a powerful agent for the transformation of others on your own or through associations with other forward-looking individuals.

Uranus in the Second House: personal finances are subjected to radical ups and downs. You may work freelance as a consultant or take short-term contractual assignments; your income fluctuates. You may earn money from the media, computers and technology, or advertising. Being resourceful in making money or cashing in on inventive ideas can sustain you economically, though you may secretly disdain money, dislike work, or work erratically just to fund creative projects.

Uranus in the Third House: an original mind, gifted at synthesis, that gets sudden inspirations or makes intuitive leaps. You may rebel against a conventional school system and prefer to be self-taught. Rather than thinking erratically or speaking compulsively, direct your mental brilliance into standup comedy, improvisation, or impromptu debates or other areas where your wit and repartee are assets.

Uranus in the Fourth House: disruptions in early life (frequent moves, a divorce, an erratic parent) that may result in your leaving home early or continuing a pattern of unsettled home life into adulthood. You may have adventuresome ancestors, or break with your family or your culture. You could continually redecorate an unusual home, or prefer not to own property at all, but, to move often, live in more than one place, or travel frequently.

Uranus in the Fifth House: dramatically and experimentally creative, using the latest techniques or technological innovations. You may love flirting and connecting with people different from you (foreigners, those of a different age, race, or social status). Your romantic life may be unstable, because you value personal freedom above emotional closeness. Any children you have may be brilliant or unusual, and you may have progressive attitudes to parenting or teaching.

Uranus in the Sixth House: interruptions in jobs or job changes. You need variety at work and may be happier working freelance or temping. You can work in technical fields (engineering or computers) with eccentric coworkers, or direct your personal need for freedom into group efforts like union organizing. Your health may be adversely affected by your nerves.

Uranus in the Seventh House: a need to balance a desire for closeness and companionship with a strong need for personal freedom. Your relationships may go through phases in which you break up and get back together repeatedly. You may prefer an unconventional situation (living together rather than legal marriage, or an open marriage, or being with a partner who comes and goes). You may gravitate to brilliant, unorthodox, or entrepreneurial partners.

Uranus in the Eighth House: investments that are subject to sudden gains and losses, or benefits coming to you from unexpected windfalls or inheritances. Your sexual charisma may lead you to explore and experiment with partners and techniques. You may want to be free from unconscious complexes related to money, sex, death, or power, and so explore innovative psychological disciplines to become free.

Uranus in the Ninth House: drawn to religions or belief systems from places distant in time or space, especially the distant past or the future, so that you create your own unique philosophy of life. You may love to travel, taking off spontaneously to explore foreign environments or charged places that are awakening and transforming. Your education may be sporadic or interrupted, and you may be drawn to study alternative or unconventional subjects.

Uranus in the Tenth House: a need for variety, challenge, and change (perhaps travel) in a career. You are happier working independently within an organization or being your own boss, perhaps as a consultant fulfilling short-term contracts. You can be creative and inventive in your field, which may be politics, public relations, the media, computers and technology, or a business with a global focus.

Uranus in the Eleventh House: attracting unusual friends with whom you have stimulating intellectual discussions about the latest news or ideas. You may have trouble integrating into groups, but ultimately find a group whose ideological bent matches yours. You can be a social gadfly, or particularly drawn to radical approaches to changing society. You can alter your goals or future directions frequently.

Uranus in the Twelfth House: interested in unusual methods of raising consciousness and experiencing altered states, possibly through drugs, unconventional spiritual practices, or occult and mystical techniques. You have a powerful creative imagination that endlessly produces images from the unconscious. You may be a secret rebel who has a deeply felt need for ultimate freedom from form.

Neptune in the Houses

The placement of Neptune by house reveals areas where you are most idealistic and sensitive. Here, you need beauty and harmony, and aspire to express perfection—but here you must be patient and realistic or risk being confused and disappointed because of false hopes. Neptune may express itself as follows:

Neptune in the First House: strong sensitivity to the environment, both physical and psychic, being highly receptive to energies of people and places. You may reflect these qualities or absorb them; in either case, setting boundaries may be difficult. You may appear beautiful, glamorous, even mysterious at times, and can make yourself almost invisible when you wish to be unnoticed. Your body may periodically experience periods of weakness or mysterious (and often temporary) symptoms requiring rest or intuitive guidance for healing.

Neptune in the Second House: idealistic about money, either having faith that you will be provided for or devaluing material things. You may be a poor judge of financial opportunities or be self-sacrificing about your salary, working for less than you merit or for the public good or for non-profit organizations. Your self-worth must be based on a spiritual core.

Neptune in the Third House: an imaginative mind, making you a good storyteller or a creative writer of poetry, plays, or fiction. You may not do well academically early on due to daydreaming or laziness, but gifts of an intuitive mind and persuasive or visionary speech can bring you success as an inspiring writer or speaker. You may have to work to bring words into focus out of the "ethers" and to be sure your ideas are yours and not adopted wholesale from others.

Neptune in the Fourth House: need for a harmonious and attractive home environment, a place of quiet retreat, possibly one where the arts are enjoyed. You may have had an imaginative, unknowable, or absent parent. Your origins may be mysterious or unclear. You may be able to access the unconscious mind easily through dreams or images, enabling you to penetrate your inner self or the hidden depths of life.

Neptune in the Fifth House: especially romantic love affairs, in which you may be either seductive or easily seduced. You may be prone to sacrificing yourself for love. A strong imagination can lead to endlessly inventive creative projects and ideas. You may idealize children as beautiful and innocent creatures. Either your own children or those you work with may be artistically gifted or sensitive and imaginative.

Neptune in the Sixth House: functioning better in a harmonious and attractive workplace. You may gravitate to charitable or non-profit companies, or health-service providers, or arts organizations. You may have to overcome a tendency to be disorganized at work, or struggle to be effective in chaotic work situations. You may suffer from mysterious health problems (like allergies, skin rashes, recurrent colds) that come and go, caused by contaminants in the environment or psychosomatic conditions.

Neptune in the Seventh House: high and sometimes unrealistic expectations about marriage and partnerships, looking for a "soulmate," a savior, or someone to fulfill your dreams and ideals. Your partner may be genuinely loving and giving, but if you have been fooled by a glamorous image, you can be disappointed by one who is undependable, deceptive, or suffering from addictions.

Neptune in the Eighth House: highly intuitive about business deals and investments *or* being duped into buying "swampland in Florida" or the Brookyn Bridge. Your sexual life can be subject to dreams and fantasies or a desire to have a deep and soulful connection with a partner. This is an excellent placement for esoteric or occult work, since you may be mediumistic, have healing abilities, or be downright psychic.

Neptune in the Ninth House: religious philosophy based on love, compassion, and selfless aid to the poor and suffering, instead of being deluded by spiritual leaders or substituting uncritical and ecstatic emotional experience for thoughtful analysis of principles. You may be uncertain about educational goals or generally subject to wishful thinking. Travel to places of spiritual significance, especially if they are near water or are foci of special energy, is beneficial.

Neptune in the Tenth House: drawn to careers in fashion or the arts, the helping or healing professions, or public service. You may easily project a glamorous image. You may be confused about your real talents and abilities, or need time to find a situation that fits them, so try to be realistic about your career goals and expectations. You may gain a high profile for charitable work or be subject to rumors and scandal (whether true or not) about your public image.

Neptune in the Eleventh House: attracting friends in the arts or helping/healing professions and working together to fundraise for charities or spiritual groups. Since you may be unclear about friends' reliability, and gullible about apparently benevolent organizations, be discriminating and investigate groups before affiliating with them. If you are confused about long-term plans, rely on intuition or gut-level instincts to guide you.

Neptune in the Twelfth House: a spiritual inheritance that enables you to tap deep inner resources through meditation, ritual work, or spiritual practices (chanting, sweat lodges, ingestion of special substances), creating a rich inner life. Strong intuition may lead you to feel spiritually guided. An overactive imagination can open you to others' fears or greater human suffering, making periodic retreats or continual psychic protection necessary.

Pluto in the Houses

Pluto's house placement shows areas you are compulsively drawn to or issues you are forced to confront, causing you to undergo significant changes. At first unconscious, powerful urges that arise bring an end to old ways of handling those affairs and inaugurate new possibilities. The key is to develop wisdom and detachment about them.

You may either express the planet's energy yourself or attract others who do. Pluto may express itself as follows:

Pluto in the First House: drawn to environments or people who try to exert power over you; in response, draw on your own determined will, depth of commitment, and radiant energy to stand up to them. Others may perceive you as a natural manager, leader, or director, and you must learn to handle their projections onto you, whether positive or negative. Recurrent health issues may force you to consider their causes: toxicity, overwork, or psychological problems.

Pluto in the Second House: an inexhaustible potential to earn income, building assets to create a secure financial foundation. You can go from rags to riches (or vice versa, if you need to overcome greed, stinginess, or an obsession with material things). You may do well to moderate your intense drive to acquire wealth and possessions and use your money to fund charitable or transformative projects for yourself.

Pluto in the Third House: a powerful mind: good at in-depth research, skilled in debating, and capable of perceptive and profound insights. Careers in public relations, politics, lobbying, media, advertising, teaching, or the law could provide outlets for mental intensity and possibly compulsive thought or speech. You may have difficulty compromising. Do not overstrain your mind or you may experience mental lapses.

Pluto in the Fourth House: draws powerful support from family, tribal, or ancestral traditions *or* a need to break free of family influences, especially if you had a domineering parent. Periodically, you may "reinvent" your home, either literally by moving or redecorating, or internally by reconceiving what home means to you. You may have an unusual ability to access the unconscious realm.

Pluto in the Fifth House: compulsive social and romantic activity, with love affairs in particular being catalysts for change. You can dig deep within yourself for creative inspiration, perhaps from ancient civilizations or mythologies, and may continually refine your artistic efforts. Your children may be strong-minded and self-disciplined and you may have difficulty asserting your authority over them, which spurs your own growth. You may be an obsessive game player, willing to risk all for love or money.

Pluto in the Sixth House: opportunities to transform (or be transformed by) your workplace. You may be obsessed with work, or deeply dissatisfied with coworkers or the working environment, to the point of protesting to management or unionizing to improve conditions. Periodically, you may need to rethink diet, nutritional needs, or lifestyle choices, as health issues will force changes. You may draw on deep healing abilities to regenerate your body.

Pluto in the Seventh House: attracting a wealthy or powerful partner who may be financially or psychologically supportive. You may have to struggle to achieve a power balance in relationships, especially if you feel trapped or dependent on a partner. Psychological work on yourself will significantly help interpersonal relations. Periodic crises can regenerate relationships, creating long-lasting bonds between devoted and passionately committed partners.

Pluto in the Eighth House: astute investments and tapping vast resources, especially for construction or renovation, though large amounts of money can come and go. You may be fascinated by taboos or secrets; wishing to unearth them can make you a talented detective, gossip columnist, archaeologist, scientist, or researcher. You may desire to probe the more esoteric secrets of birth, death, and the afterlife. You can either draw on others' energies or regenerate them through powerful healing energy. An intense sexuality may lead to exploring taboos or magical practices.

Pluto in the Ninth House: struggles with beliefs, during which you encounter religions and philosophies (or powerful and charismatic teachers and gurus) that powerfully shape your world view. You are capable of passionately defending your ideas or trying to influence others to adopt them. You may travel to places of spiritual power, or have transforming experiences while traveling. You can apply your intense mind to in-depth educational studies, especially psychology or business and finance.

Pluto in the Tenth House: a powerful force in the world, especially in politics or business. You need to be in a position of authority where you can make a difference, and perhaps create financial opportunities for both yourself and your employer. Be ethical in your career or you can trigger powerful opposition or a fall from grace. You can regenerate your own career as well as revamp the companies that hire you.

Pluto in the Eleventh House: powerful and influential friends who are agents of change for you. Friendships may bring struggles, but surviving much together can create deep and lasting bonds. You can affiliate with organizations determined to change society, possibly by helping the poor or oppressed, or join secret societies. You can be the group's recognized leader, whether elected or not, and be especially good at fundraising.

Pluto in the Twelfth House: opening up powerful sources of comfort and aid through direct connection to the unconscious (in psychological terms) or the divine (in religious language). You can draw on the collective wisdom of your ancestors or of the whole human race. Initially you may have difficulty accessing your power. Periods of silence or retreat, or intense therapy during which you face your personal dark side or humanity's shadow, or extreme methods of altering consciousness can release energy and power.

CHAPTER FOUR

ASPECTS: THE FOURTH PIECE

As PLANETS GLIDE AROUND THE SUN, they move periodically into certain pre-defined geometric relationships to one another. These geometrical relationships are called "aspects." They link together two or more planetary energies to create much of the horoscope's dynamism. When you calculate the natal chart, you look for aspects active at the moment of birth. Patterns created by these connections, whether cooperative or stressful, reveal the psyche's inner structure and significantly describe personality drives, life themes, and potential events. Aspects occur not only between planets, but between planets and other important points, like the Ascendant and Midheaven.

Aspects are derived by dividing the 360-degree circle by whole numbers between one and twelve. They are interpreted by drawing on number theory going back to Pythagoras. In many cultures (Babylonian, Hindu, Greek, Chinese) and religions (Buddhist, Jewish, Christian, Islamic), numbers are fundamental principles from which the world emerged and thus are prominent religious symbols, a sacred and secret language in their own right. For Greek philosophers as well as modern esotericists, numbers are the beginnings of all things, creating the perfect "music of the spheres" that underlies creation.

To calculate aspects (in non-technical terms), we measure the angular distance between planets in degrees along the ecliptic (the Sun's apparent path around Earth).

To understand aspects, you must have a good grasp of the planets' nature and combine that comprehension with the aspect's symbolism. Here is where deeper chart analysis begins. While separate interpretations of planets in signs and houses are meaningful, aspects show how they are reinforced or modified. Aspects also point to which of the many potential manifestations of the planetary energies are more likely than others.

Aspects are classified as either MAJOR or MINOR. Major aspects have been part of astrological tradition since at least Ptolemy (2nd century C.E.). They are considered more powerful than minor

			Table 3. Table of Aspects		
Division Number	Symbol	Name	Exact Degree	Classification	Quality
1	☌	conjunction	0°	major	depends on planets involved
2	☍	opposition	180°	major	disharmonious
3	△	trine	120°	major	harmonious
4	♄ or □	square	90°	major	disharmonious
5	✫	quintile	72°	minor	harmonious
6	✶	sextile	60°	major	harmonious
8	∠	semi-square	45°	minor	disharmonious
12	⊻	semi-sextile	30°	minor	depends on planets involved
3 x 8	⬚	sesqui-quadrate	135°	minor	disharmonious
5 x 12	⊼	quincunx (or inconjunct)	150°	minor	disharmonious

aspects, some of which were introduced by mathematician/astrologer Johannes Kepler in the early 17th century. All twelve known aspects are currently being reexamined, principally because of John Addey's work in England on aspects and harmonic theory.

More obscure aspects (sevenths, ninths, tenths, and elevenths) are thought to indicate unusual abilities, spiritual talents, or potentials of such high frequency that few can tap them, so they are rarely used in Western astrology.

Aspects are also interpreted as either HARMONIOUS (easy) or DISHARMONIOUS (stressful) according to their number series. To illustrate: aspects resulting from the circle's division by 3 (or 6 or 12) are considered *harmonious* or *easy*, while those deriving from division by 2 (or 4 or 8) are considered *disharmonious* or *hard*. In numerology, the number three relates to ease, stability, and resolution, while the number two refers to division and polarity, hence challenge.

There is a catch-22 here: although harmonious aspects show abilities that come easily to the person, they often do not manifest their potential or take advantage of opportunities; and while hard aspects are usually stressful and obstructive, they often provide motivation to overcome difficulties and build character, develop skills, and achieve success. A balance of easy and hard is better. Aspects blend harmonies and cacophonies, creating the "music of the soul."

Aspects are rarely exact (for example, precisely ninety degrees), so we allow a certain "give or take," a range on either side within which the two planets must fall in order to be "in aspect." This deviation is called the ORB. Different astrologers use larger or smaller orbs to gauge where the aspect is thought to begin and end. I personally use wider orbs, as people with a higher level of awareness will pull them in. My suggestions for orb allowance are given below when I discuss the individual aspects. As a general rule, the farther away the planets are from each other around the wheel (like 120 or 180 degrees), the wider the allowable orb.

The closer the orb of the aspect by degree, the more strongly its presence is felt. Aspects that are APPLYING or approaching exactitude (i.e., when the planets are moving closer to each other), are considered more powerful, and imply that issues inherent in them *must* be dealt with in this lifetime. SEPARATING aspects of wider orb (i.e., when the planets are moving apart from each other), are thought to be waning, relating to the past, and less influential over time.

Sometimes you can easily see aspects in a chart. Planets having the same degree number in their respective signs are undoubtedly in aspect. Planets that fall withn the same element (earth, air, fire, or water—thus four signs apart) may be in trine. If they have the same quality (cardinal, fixed, or mutable—thus three signs apart), they may be in square. Check the degree numbers to see if they fall into the allowable orb, or simply refer to a computer-generated aspect table. These days computers will do all the work of calculating aspects, listing their degree distances, and indicating whether they are applying or separating. You can set the program for whatever orbs you wish to use.

Major Aspects

Conjunction (0°) OR CIRCLE DIVIDED BY 1: ORB USUALLY BETWEEN 8° AND 10°: Energies are fused and intensified, and modify each other; they must work together whether compatible or different in nature. The combined meaning relates to the symbolism of number one: the seed of a new cycle, the original unity that engenders the next numbers.

Opposition (180°) OR CIRCLE DIVIDED BY 2: ORB USUALLY BETWEEN 8° AND 10°: This represents the fundamental polarity or duality arising at the moment of creation when the undifferentiated One of the mystical traditions becomes two (manifesting in all pairs of opposites). It creates tension leading to frustration, though objectivity can lead to a delicate balancing of opposites. Oppositions are often projected as outer circumstances or individuals who block your way. Resolving the tension is helped by opposing factors often having the same quality. Energies can bounce back and forth—or compromise— through awareness that two halves are in essence a whole.

Trine (120°) OR CIRCLE DIVIDED BY 3: ORB USUALLY BETWEEN 8° AND 10°: Connecting signs of the same element, this is the easiest expression of linked energies. Trines connote luck and opportunities as well as innate creative talents, though these may be taken for granted and not expressed. The relationship between the linked energies is the most harmonious possible and tends to manifest the most pleasant potential. The number three is a "heavenly" number, alluding to the soul, represented by the self-contained Trinity, and symbolized by the tripod's equilibrium.

Square (90°) OR CIRCLE DIVIDED BY 4: ORB USUALLY BETWEEN 8° AND 10°: A square encompasses one-fourth of the circle, with four being the number signifying Earth, the plane of solid manifestation represented by the cube. It implies the inherent restrictions and resistances of matter and time. A square is dynamic, and creates challenges that pressure you to work on the issues represented by the planets involved. Energies are at cross-purposes; conflict leads to irritation; achievement is delayed, though patient hard work can lead to success through integration of the two principles.

Sextile (60°) OR CIRCLE DIVIDED BY 6: ORB TO 6°: The sextile also indicates talents or opportunities, but is more likely to find an outlet than the trine. The ancient philosopher Philo calls it the "most productive of all numbers." The energies in a sextile collaborate well and work comfortably together. Its inherent balance is depicted in Solomon's Seal, two interlocking triangles containing six sextiles. Six is the number of perfect balance.

Minor Aspects

Quintile (72°) OR CIRCLE DIVIDED BY 5: ORB 2–3°: The number five is preeminently the "number of humanity," symbolized by our reliance on the five senses. It refers to reason as the divine faculty, distinguishing human beings from animals. Quintiles imply artistic or creative talents, especially mental ones, as well as versatility and an authentic individuality.

Semi-square (45°) OR CIRCLE DIVIDED BY 8, and **Sesqui-quadrate (135° WHICH IS 5/8 OF THE CIRCLE): ORB FOR SEMI-SQUARE: 2–3°; FOR SESQUIQUADRATE (A SQUARE AND A HALF): 3–4°:** Both of these aspects are variations on the square and part of the 2/4/8 series. These imply friction, generating minor conflict or frustration that can be annoying. Semi-squares may correlate more with internal conflict, while sesqui-quadrates seem more likely to externalize difficulties.

Semi-sextile (30°) OR CIRCLE DIVIDED BY 12: ORB OF 2–3°: Once thought mildly beneficent, this aspect may actually be awkward or mildly difficult. As one twelfth of the circle, it participates in the harmonious series related to multiples of 3, but because it connects signs of different elements and qualities, it seems uncomfortable.

Quincunx or Inconjunct (150°) OR 5/12 OF THE CIRCLE: ORB OF 3°–4°: This aspect vacillates between acting like a trine and acting like an opposition, so it demands continual adjustments and balances. The stress it creates may have health implications. The irritation inherent in the quincunx may derive from the lack of commonality between linked factors; they are different in both element and quality.

Aspects can actually be seen as parts of astronomical cycles that begin with the conjunction of two planets. Over time, all the planets will form every aspect with each other, as the faster-moving planets progress around the zodiacal circle ahead of the slower. Thus, two planets will reunite at another conjunction days, months, or years later.

Planets in Aspect

The following interpretations are clustered under two headings. Harmonious aspects include trine, sextile, and sometimes conjunction. Disharmonious aspects include opposition, square, semi-square, sesqui-quadrate, quincunx, and sometimes conjunction. Categorizing the conjunction depends greatly on the two planets connected. Generally, any aspect between a planet and Venus or Jupiter can be friendly; the principal danger is in overdoing.

Not all of the possibilities in one category will describe your experience, so try to be objective about which ones apply. Actually, you may feel that parts of *both* harmonious and disharmonious descriptions fit you, no matter which aspect you have in your chart. Even if you have a disharmonious connection, statements in that section may have been true for you only when you were younger. You may have "graduated" into a more harmonious expression as you have matured. If you do have stressful combinations, use the conflict as positively and productively as you can to spur your growth and learning. Changing your behaviors or attitudes can help transform challenges into strengths.

Aspects to the Sun

SUN-MOON

Harmonious: comfortably joins masculine and feminine energies, so you are emotionally stable and well balanced; emotional needs harmonize with outer circumstances; good relations with family and partners; parents may have been compatible; unconscious needs support life goals and career initiatives.

Disharmonious: may feel restless and dissatisfied; unconscious programming derails efforts; emotional tension with parents or partners originates in childhood experiences; you feel a disjunction between inner feelings and outer circumstances.

SUN-MERCURY

Mercury can never be more than twenty-eight degrees from the Sun, so the only aspects possible are the conjunction and semi-sextile. The closer Mercury is to the Sun, the harder it is to be detached and impersonal in your thinking, though it often indicates a career related to language or communication skills. Mercury in a sign different from the Sun broadens your outlook.

SUN-VENUS

Venus is never more than forty-eight degrees from the Sun, so only the conjunction, semi-sextile, and semi-square can form between the two.

Harmonious: identity based on loving and being loved; gives popularity, warmth, charm, refinement, social ease, and possibly artistic flair; attracts people, wealth, and pleasant life circumstances; needs peace and harmony.

Disharmonious: may be seductive and manipulative; overly sensual and fond of luxuries and ease; vain, self-centered, and lazy.

Sun-Mars

Harmonious: gives energy and dynamism to achieve goals; capable of taking action and being decisive as a leader; self-confident and ambitious; may be the adventurer or warrior constantly seeking new challenges.

Disharmonious: restless, impatient, and easily frustrated, causing impulsive actions or foolish risk-taking; competitive; may be excessively sexual; problems controlling temper lead to conflicts with others; potentially destructive to self (overwork) and others (aggression); personality dominated by masculine side.

Sun-Jupiter

Harmonious: a gentle, generous, kind disposition; tolerant and easygoing; a positive attitude attracts opportunities (that seem lucky); career expands more and more successfully over time, and is especially gratifying if it encompasses learning and adventure; may be multi-talented.

Disharmonious: restless and easily bored; energy dissipated in too many directions; always wants more and is never satisfied, though it may overindulge and overspend; pompous and preachy; lazy and self-satisfied.

Sun-Saturn

Harmonious: patient and hardworking, allowing confidence and success to build slowly through sustained effort; likely to be serious and mature at an early age; takes on adult responsibilities and discharges them conscientiously; gives strength and endurance; success and self-acceptance come late in life.

Disharmonious: slow to develop; may be rigid, inhibited at first; a late bloomer; suffers from workaholism; has a poor relationship with parents (likely father), authorities, government; must overcome difficult childhood or physical limitations or low self-esteem by gaining others' respect due to career achievement and money earned; with emotional and financial security, life opens up.

SUN-URANUS

Harmonious: a creative, inventive, progressive, daring, and unconventional character that needs literal and emotional freedom; possible mental brilliance or unusual perceptive abilities lead to feeling displaced; life and career may involve media, travel, or alternative approaches, especially as a pioneer or catalyst for cultural change; periodically, career mutates or changes unexpectedly.

Disharmonious: restless, erratic, eccentric, and so unable to integrate into a group; reacts by being stubborn, difficult, and compulsively obstinate; may be a disruptive force or experience interruptions in career that undermine long-term success; change is upsetting.

SUN-NEPTUNE

Harmonious: sensitive, imaginative, and intuitive, with serious interests in mysticism and spirituality or the arts (especially acting); highly adaptable, and "goes with the flow"; career may be in the helping/healing or service professions where energy is easily directed to others; has a talent for working with dreams, myths, and images.

Disharmonious: lack of clarity about yourself and your talents can lead to confusion about life path; if identity not based on soul or spirit, naiveté, ungroundedness, and extreme sensitivity can lead to being lost in dreams and fantasies or seeking escape in drugs or alcohol; can be self-deluded or fooled by others.

SUN-PLUTO

Harmonious: determined, focused, and intense; you may have strong will and ambition leading to promotions and prosperity; periodically, you and your life undergo transformations that are handled well due to inner strength, survival ability, and resourcefulness; can build an empire or midwife others' evolution, facilitating their growth and success along with your own.

Disharmonious: may initially feel dominated and helpless, and must reclaim power to use for your own as well as others' benefit, instead of manipulating or exploiting them; initially stubborn, willful, and resistant to change, you may need to master yourself (overcoming addictions or obsessive/compulsive behavior) before challenging others; may take the modern "hero's journey" into your own unconscious or the past to grow psychologically; may be forced to redirect power from the ego to the higher self.

Aspects to the Moon

MOON-MERCURY

Harmonious: easily expresses feelings in words; good memory; quickly sizes up people and situations and responds realistically; reasoning supports emotional needs; mental statements (mantras, affirmations) align with emotions.

Disharmonious: nervous tension and restlessness; head and heart conflict, so you can talk yourself out of what you want, or allow others to do so; needs are frustrated by apparently sensible decisions.

MOON-VENUS

Harmonious: harmony between emotional and social circumstances; popularity due to warmth, charm, and sympathetic nature; many good friends, especially women, who provide benefits.

Disharmonious: emotional neediness interferes with personal happiness; conflict between inner child's immature wishes and more adult social demands; may feel uncomfortable in social situations.

MOON-MARS

Harmonious: has energized emotions; has warmth, passion, and emotional daring; can defend home, family, and country as the warrior, motivated by strongly protective feelings; has sex appeal.

Disharmonious: impulsive and prone to emotional outbursts; may be defensive *or* aggressive in starting conflicts; argumentative and confrontational; carries unconscious or conscious anger at mother, family, or restrictions on personal life, hence difficulties with women, children, or childbirth; would benefit from anger-management courses.

MOON-JUPITER

Harmonious: positive, optimistic, and confident; emotionally open and tolerant; liked by and receives benefits from women, family, and public; likes a pleasant, spacious home; liked by others for genial nature; gains emotional satisfaction from religion, philosophy, meta-physics; has faith in the Universe.

Disharmonious: emotional responses are exaggerated; lazy, restless, and always wanting more; never satisfied; spoiled, indulged and indulgent; has no emotional backbone; is emotionally effusive but insincere; likes situations to be easy.

MOON-SATURN

Harmonious: emotionally reserved; emotions are disciplined to be patient, prudent, and responsible; can plan long-term to achieve emotional satisfaction; has few friends but they are loyal, stable, and often older; women provide security and stability.

Disharmonious: emotionally repressed and depressed; can overcome difficulties with parents (especially mother) or childhood restrictions by patient work; public stiffness covers up fears and insecurities; self-protective; may overwork; builds confidence through work and others' respect for their contributions to society.

MOON-URANUS

Harmonious: open and flexible, so can accept changes; can balance needs for intimacy and expression of individuality, though prefers to feel emotionally free; may have an unusual childhood, mother, or home life; finds creative or humanitarian activities emotionally satisfying.

Disharmonious: can alternately repress or blurt out feelings; takes risks or disrupts relationships or home life due to feeling constrained or seeking excitement; nervous and emotionally erratic, with mood swings to the point of noticeable instability and social ostracism.

MOON-NEPTUNE

Harmonious: sensitive, empathic, and compassionate; needs peace and refinement in home and social life; has strong intuition and mystical tendencies; romantic and idealistic; can create beauty due to innately sensing harmony, balance, and proportion.

Disharmonious: experiences emotional confusion and dissatisfaction leading to escapism or problems with addictions; self-deceived or deceived by others due to naiveté or gullibility, or unrealistic expectations; easily seduced; may be disappointed by unreliable friends or partners.

MOON-PLUTO

Harmonious: emotionally intense; can channel charged feelings into creative pursuits; can easily access unconscious complexes and clear them, leading to psychological growth; a natural psychologist or human resources person; can understand and motivate others.

Disharmonious: stubborn, rigid, and controlling in order to feel safe; early in life may experience powerful and overwhelming dark emotions (like rage, jealousy, resentment, and vengefulness) that are repressed, often leading to obsessive/compulsive behaviors; resistant to confronting and transmuting negative emotions to generosity, love, and forgiveness.

Aspects to Mercury

MERCURY-VENUS

Mercury and Venus are never more than seventy-two degrees apart, so possible aspects between them are conjunction, semi-sextile, semi-square, sextile, and quintile.

Harmonious: has charming, persuasive speech; easily impresses others and elicits a positive response to ideas; writing comes easily; can converse with anyone socially; tactful and diplomatic; loves to learn.

Disharmonious: may say what will flatter or what the other person wants to hear; insincere and hypocritical; wants only pleasant conversation and dislikes arguing.

MERCURY-MARS

Harmonious: quick mind that grasps ideas and their implications instantly, often bypassing logic; sharp, perceptive, and precise thinking; physical dexterity, and can act quickly, especially in a crisis; may be witty and satirical; a mental fighter and good in debate.

Disharmonious: quick-tempered, quick to take offense; has a sarcastic, cutting, and cruel tongue; a harsh critic; talks nonstop, interrupting others; ideas are egotistically oriented.

MERCURY-JUPITER

Harmonious: broadminded, tolerant, optimistic, and liberal in out-look; sees the grand overview; has a naturally philosophical mind; curious, loves to expand knowledge and be exposed to unfamiliar areas of study, so learns easily; likes mental freedom.

Disharmonious: affected by impractical and ungrounded thinking that ignores facts or realities; tries to explore too much, literally or intellectually; finds it hard to express thoughts clearly in words; mind is restless and easily distracted; mentally lazy; exaggerates; thoughts have no depth; sees conflict between reason and faith.

MERCURY-SATURN

Harmonious: a disciplined, precise, serious, and conservative thinker; has writing ability for non-fiction, scientific papers, and in-depth research; has good budgeting and planning skills, particularly long-term; thinks slowly, but clearly and logically.

Disharmonious: pedantic, labored thinking; feels intellectually inade-quate and may be an insecure speaker; has difficulty expressing ideas, from lack of confidence, limited vocabulary, lack of schooling, men-tal blocks, or learning disabilities.

MERCURY-URANUS

Harmonious: brilliant, insightful thinking; can synthesize ideas, make connections, and solve problems; progressive and embraces alternative perspectives or unusual approaches; may have interest in esoteric, cross-cultural, or futuristic ideas.

Disharmonious: an erratic thinker who jumps to illogical conclu-sions; responds impulsively and impatiently; brain and nervous sys-tem are over-stimulated; can entertain fixed, impractical, or extreme ideas, and often argues them just to upset people.

MERCURY-NEPTUNE

Harmonious: can balance intellect and intuition; an imaginative thinker and natural storyteller who can write fiction, plays, poetry; moves with physical grace; uses images to stimulate thoughts; has psychic or mediumistic ability.

Disharmonious: subject to impractical or wishful thinking; may use language to deceive, seduce, or downright lie; may stay silent, be incoherent, or substitute jargon or clichés for real communication; experiences dissociated or delusional thinking when the mind disconnects from "reality."

MERCURY-PLUTO

Harmonious: an intense mind that can maintain a sustained focus on an idea or mental project; has mental power that can be used to influence or persuade in advertising, education, politics, or public relations; has penetrating perception that can expose others' motives or secrets.

Disharmonious: mental overwork can strain the mind to the point of exhaustion or breakdown—so take breaks from work; can use mind power to manipulate or hypnotize others; may have fixed, negative, obsessive ideas that are outdated, unreasonable, or prejudiced and hard to change.

Aspects to Venus

VENUS-MARS

Harmonious: attractive, sexually magnetic, and passionate; readily enters into friendships and relationships; integrates cooperation and self-assertion to sustain popularity; easily generates money through efforts.

Disharmonious: experiences disappointments because of impulsive social connections that are on and off or short-term; alienates others by making demands or placing ego needs first; loves to seduce, but ultimately finds conquests empty.

VENUS-JUPITER

Harmonious: warm, friendly, outgoing, and affectionate, so has many friends and busy social life; materially protected, so can be generous and philanthropic; easily expresses artistic talents or loves the arts.

Disharmonious: a social butterfly, never developing deeper connections; extravagant and self-indulgent, overspending on unnecessary luxuries to impress; has high expectations, but is lazy and may expect friends and partners to provide material support.

VENUS-SATURN

Harmonious: loyal and dependable in fewer, but longer-term, friendships; is attracted to older or emotionally mature individuals; repays security with being responsible and performing the conventional role well; prefers simplicity and quality in the arts.

Disharmonious: attracted to cold, withholding, rejecting partners, so that disappointments in love lead to withdrawal and self-denial; fears poverty and distrusts others, so is miserly with money and affection; feels socially awkward and unfashionable; personal happiness is delayed until fears and defenses are overcome.

VENUS-URANUS

Harmonious: gets along with anyone: foreigners, older or younger people, and those of different racial, religious, or social backgrounds, so is a "global citizen"; has unusual friends and an adventuresome social life; can be popular because of daring behavior or outrageous comments (like certain comedians); artistically original.

Disharmonious: friendships and relationships are disrupted by unpredictable, unconventional, or unacceptable behavior; finds it hard to make and sustain commitments due to need for freedom; disdains conventional roles and expectations; money is erratic.

VENUS-NEPTUNE

Harmonious: loving, sympathetic, and compassionate, so can harmonize with anyone; can appreciate the inner beauty of the soul in everyone; love of the divine; romantic and idealistic in love, seeking a soulmate with whom you have unspoken empathy; refined feelings and taste, with an innate style; a strong imagination gives artistic talent; can attract "magic money."

Disharmonious: nebulous friendships; relationships may have more fantasy than reality; delusions about a partner or partner's commitment; taken in by a glamorous image or oblivious to partner's addictions to drugs or alcohol; impractical with money.

VENUS-PLUTO

Harmonious: desire for deep, committed, and intimate relationships (bonded "until death do you part") that can be continually renewed and re-energized; personal connections are catalysts for growth and self-transformation; erotic magnetism; has boundless creativity; feels a need for intense and passionate sexual experiences; can generate and regenerate resources/money.

Disharmonious: has serious, often unconscious, power issues in relationships, often manipulating through guilt, domination, or keeping partner dependent through fear of loss; compulsively and insatiably sexual; exploits others for money; goes to emotional extremes; obsessed by negative feelings (jealousy, resentment, hatred), but may hide these instead of transmuting them into more positive ones.

Aspects to Mars

MARS-JUPITER

Harmonious: magnifies energies so there is a high level of enthusiasm, exuberance, and physical drive; can be continually active or athletic, using sports for self-improvement; a natural crusader, often fighting for faith or justice.

Disharmonious: energies are scattered in frantically trying to do too much, leading to alternating periods of overdrive and inertia; over-confidence can lead to taking physical risks or gambling; can argue about belief systems; may overindulge sensually.

MARS-SATURN

Harmonious: energy is disciplined and directed; capable of working long and hard on projects, with the patience and stamina to complete them despite delays or obstacles; you may get physically stronger as you get older.

Disharmonious: feels deep resentment and frustration when desires or drives are delayed or blocked by authorities, circumstances, or timing; repressed energy can trigger an explosive temper or violence; sexual mistiming or inhibitions; sexual repression can find socially unacceptable outlets.

MARS-URANUS

Harmonious: energy is easily excited and channeled into unusual activities, possibly social reform, technological inventions, or original actions; needs a variety of interests, and can easily multi-task; sexually experimental.

Disharmonious: energy is scattered and output is erratic; high-strung and restless, so hard to maintain a routine and cooperate with others due to "conceited independence"; takes physical risks and may be accident-prone; may be a protester or revolutionary.

MARS-NEPTUNE

Harmonious: physical grace and ease plus a sense of rhythm find outlets in dance or aesthetic sports (like synchronized swimming); motivated by idealism and inspiration to be a "spiritual warrior" and participate in activities like peace movements or environmental activism; imagination directs energies into arts or spiritual quests.

Disharmonious: energies wax and wane mysteriously, leading to inertia and passivity; can be confused about goals and intentions, and deluded about accomplishments; actions can be impractical or unfocused; indulges in sexual fantasy.

MARS-PLUTO

Harmonious: tremendous energy reserves, enabling sustained periods of focused work before resting and recharging batteries; dedicated, determined, and persistent to succeed; passionate and sexually intense; uses personal energies for collective good, so can catalyze transformations of individuals or the community.

Disharmonious: relentless drive can lead to burnout; obstinate, willful, and rigid in focus on goals and may force others to collaborate; compulsively sexual, often driven to push boundaries and explore taboos; power can be used destructively, in subversiveness, bad temper, or violence.

Aspects to Jupiter

JUPITER-SATURN

Harmonious: has excellent business sense in planning strategically, timing moves well, and building a firm foundation for stable, steady growth; can apply religious principles practically, based on both firm faith and deep understanding.

Disharmonious: mistimes efforts, starting new ventures without completing the old; experiences ethical, moral, or religious conflicts because of uncertainty about beliefs; alternates between optimism and pessimism, satisfaction and dissatisfaction.

JUPITER-URANUS

Harmonious: encounters luck and opportunities for growth, wealth, and success, facilitated by a positive attitude and faith in outcomes; may have original and inventive ideas, with an intuitive feel for making right choices; wants freedom to explore possibilities and have adventures.

Disharmonious: takes chances, gambling or acting recklessly; has grand ideas, but may be unable to focus; expects a positive outcome without effort; may be either dogmatic or discontented with beliefs; has interest in unusual religions or philosophies, but tends not to stay with one path.

JUPITER-NEPTUNE

Harmonious: genuinely spiritual: kind, compassionate, pure in heart; loves philosophical and spiritual explorations, and finds opportunities to grow in grace; intuition is magnified; may be motivated to help and heal, use the imagination in artistic ways, or travel as a spiritual seeker.

Disharmonious: spiritually gullible, deluded, or confused, so dissatisfied with any path, which may lead to various forms of escapism; may try too many religious or spiritual approaches and get "spiritual indigestion"; foolishly impractical; has an exaggerated sensitivity and tends toward sentimentality.

JUPITER-PLUTO

Harmonious: luck blends with ambition and determination to create material success; finds the easy way to personal power; seeks powerful philosophies that are transforming; will dig and fight for truth; can refine lower nature through application of ethical principles; can teach powerfully.

Disharmonious: has grand ambitions and desires, especially for power over others, but may overwork or be frustrated by outcomes; strives to build an empire, possibly on an unethical foundation; mis-uses knowledge to exploit others for gain.

Aspects to Saturn

SATURN-URANUS

Harmonious: can innovate steadily within established situations if given some flexibility; balances responsibilities and freedom; can bridge past and future, combining traditional and modern; can organize reform movements.

Disharmonious: conflict between parental or social restrictions and intense desire for independence generates tension leading to erratic behavior, compulsive rebelliousness, or violent eruptions; fears the new.

SATURN-NEPTUNE

Harmonious: the practical idealist or constructive artist who can manifest visions and dreams; makes steady spiritual progress as a grounded mystic, even within conventional religion; can "go with the flow" without losing focus.

Disharmonious: has difficulty actualizing goals, making ideals work-able, and bringing dreams into reality; may be fooled by fraudulent religious or spiritual groups; may become sad or frustrated by humanity's imperfections, the material world's limits, or longing for an impossible Utopia.

SATURN-PLUTO

Harmonious: builds slowy and strategically to achieve lasting wealth and success; revamps projects or regenerates institutions to give them new life; has endurance, will power, and determination to survive crises and emerge stronger.

Disharmonious: life may be periodically derailed by circumstances beyond your control, so you have to keep starting over; tension and frustration build due to deep dissatisfaction with yourself and soci-ety, leading to attacks on authority; may be stubborn, bullying, harsh, or cruel.

Aspects to Uranus

URANUS-NEPTUNE

Harmonious: intuition and imagination are powerfully linked, generating insightful dreaming; may be genuinely spiritually gifted: visionary, charismatic, compassionate, and unusually perceptive; may have psychic gifts or artistic brilliance; may transform spiritual groups, seek to harmonize religions, or start a new one altogether.

Disharmonious: has a confused desire for change and misplaced idealism, so may become involved in short-lived reform movements or unethical religious organizations; may use drugs to alter awareness; may experience muddled thinking and rationalize unethical behavior.

URANUS-PLUTO

Harmonious: wants immediate and powerful revolutionary change; has inventive ideas for transforming people and improving culture and environment; has insights into power and authority or people's psyches.

Disharmonious: personal life goes through periodic dramatic upheavals; your historical time period is disrupted and chaotic (revolutions, assassinations, wars); uncontrollable changes create tremendous inner pressure, leading to rebelliousness, willful and resentful misuse of power, and violent destructiveness.

Aspects to Neptune

NEPTUNE-PLUTO

Harmonious: a profound interest in religious, spiritual, and occult topics, especially pre-birth and afterlife states; emotionally intense, and consequently motivated to grow psychologically; has access to true spiritual power and charisma, with possible healing ability; driven to transform religions, dissolve power structures, or break up impediments to progress.

Disharmonious: experiences confusion, conflict, and crises in religious matters, possibly being manipulated or defrauded by religious groups; may be fanatical about beliefs, seduced by fantasies of spiritual power, or overwhelmed by unconscious drives and hence "possessed"; may be driven by obsessions, compulsions, and delusions.

Aspect Patterns

A horoscope can have many aspects of one harmonic type. For instance, many squares (or semi-squares or sesqui-quadrates) lend much dynamism and abundant challenges. Three or more planets can also be linked to form complex geometric shapes and patterns, which heightens their energetic quality. For example, trines can join hands to form "grand trines," while squares can lock into T-squares or even grand squares. (See diagrams of major configurations on page 121.) The more planets that plug into the configuration, the stronger the effect and the more the pattern dominates the chart and colors the personality.

There are many different aspect configurations. The following six are especially important.

Stellium

Technically, a stellium is four or more planets in one sign (though some astrologers will accept three), often close enough to be overlapping conjunctions. You can also have a stellium by house. This configuration is one giant bundle of energy, with each planet inescapably tied to the others. The key word for a stellium is "intensity." Having many planets in one sign gives it extra weight in the horoscope, and can mean that the traits associated with that sign have a strong presence in the personality. With so many energies connected, interpreting this can be challenging. First look at the sign in which the stellium falls. Then decide which planet is dominant, either being well placed by sign and house or making aspects that others do not.

Grand Trine

When three trines link to form an equilateral triangle, the energy moves easily and harmoniously between them, since they likely have a common element. However, the same dilemma persists with a grand trine as with a single one: the energies are in a self-contained loop and not challenged to grow and change. However, if the grand trine includes dynamic planets like Mars, Saturn, or Pluto, pressure may manifest the trine's positive qualities. Tighter orbs between the connected planets also give greater potential for externalization. If other, more dynamic aspects connect to points of the grand trine, this also energizes it. The grand trine should still signify talents or luck; the necessity is to prod them into action.

Kite

Grand trines are much likelier to express themselves if the pattern contains an opposition to one of the planets, creating a kite shape, with two sextiles linking the opposition to the trines. This is because the opposition forces action and provides a dynamic outlet for the energies.

T-Square

This common pattern is found when two planets oppose each other and are square (ninety degrees) a third, which may be the outlet for frustrated energy. Sometimes the pattern increases difficulties since three rather than two planets now conflict, but the opposition can provide some perspective on handling the energies. Look carefully at the third planet, square to the two ends, for clues about how to deal with the tension. With a lot of drive inherent in the squares, the person with this pattern can focus great energy to overcome obstacles and achieve much.

Grand Square (or Grand Cross)

The T-square becomes a grand square with the addition of a fourth planet at right angles to *both* ends. This creates a box shape of four squares, with the corners joined by oppositions. With two oppositions plus four squares—all in a state of heightened tension because elements conflict—you can indeed feel "boxed in" with this pattern. Such a tremendous amount of linked energy can enable you to accomplish much and be highly creative. The planets in this configuration are usually in signs of the same quality. The most difficult grand square is in fixed signs, as the planets' potencies can be resistant to change. Look for easy aspects to any point of the grand square to offer outlets.

Yod

This pattern has two quincunxes connected to a sextile, which puts stress on issues related to the planets involved. Because quincunxes require adjustment, you are constantly reevaluating your priorities. Fortunately, the sextile can provide opportunities for resolving crises in which you have to face facts and alter course. Some believe that a yod portends a special task to perform in life.

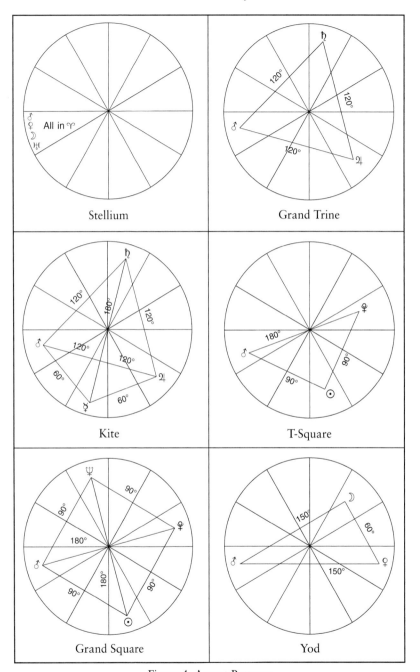

Figure 4. Aspect Patterns

Part Two:

The Practical Application

CHAPTER FIVE

UNDERSTANDING A CHART

Now we come to the "art" of astrology—the synthesis of all the pieces—that allows you to deduce your character and destiny. "Synthesizing" means combining separate elements or substances into a coherent whole. In this case, you combine the essential meanings of the planets, placed in particular signs, in specific houses, and making certain aspects to each other. This is facilitated by a three-step process. Oprah Winfrey's chart on page 128 will serve as an example to take us through the steps. Her birth data is accurate (verified by her on television and substantiated on the important website for accurate birth data, *www.astrodatabank.com*). Her public status allows us to look at her life without violating client confidentiality.

Step One: Get a "Feel" for the Whole
Since the chart *is* initially a whole, first scan it to get an overall picture. This draws on the right side of the brain, the one that intuitively and spontaneously gets the "gestalt." The right brain cannot verbalize what it knows; instead, it absorbs meaning wordlessly through references to the senses, metaphors, symbols, and images. Since astrology is a language of symbols, the principal one being the circle itself, it innately appeals to this brain hemisphere. Horoscopes printed in color can also help engage the right brain. These immediately communicate the energetic quality of planetary connections (red for squares and oppositions, for instance) and highlight aspect patterns. Computer-generated charts can be printed in color, or you can draw aspect lines yourself with colored pencils.

To engage this perceptive part of your mind, just sit and look at the horoscope without actively thinking about it. Let your mind go into meditative mode. Be attentive, but non-directive. What stands out to you? Where do you see emphases? In certain signs or houses? In elements or qualities? In prominent planets or attention-getting aspect patterns?

Look for contradictions, because these help form bridges to the more creative right brain. One of the appealing aspects of astrology is that paradoxes abound—this is precisely what makes human beings such complex and intriguing creatures. What happens when there are contradictions? They do not cancel each other out. You either need to make difficult choices between different options or integrate competing drives, conflicting interests, and opposing needs. Sometimes simply alternating between ways of being or doing will satisfy different parts of you; sometimes it is possible to blend them. These contradictions describe both inner dilemmas and outer circumstances.

Step Two: Analyze the Parts

Next, take the chart apart to examine each separate piece, as if you were taking a watch apart to see how it works. This follows the scientific method originated by the Greeks: "analysis precedes synthesis." Doing this engages your left brain—the one that is logical and verbal, analytic and sequential, able to focus on separate facts. While your left brain is kept busy doing the analysis, your right brain can still make connections subliminally.

With all the information packed into a horoscope, using a worksheet can be helpful. The one featured here was created by me following Richard Idemon's method, which he briefly explains in *Through the Looking Glass: A Search for the Self in the Mirror of Relationships*. (On pages 221–224, he applies the method to Isadora Duncan's chart). Idemon varied his system over the years, but I have stayed with his original idea of assigning fifteen points to major chart factors. I have also added to the worksheet. You too can add to or subtract from this as you learn more about astrology.

First, allot points: one for each planet in the chart, two each for the Sun and Moon, one for the planet that rules the sign on the Ascendant, and one each for the Ascendant and Midheaven signs. The total will be fifteen, except for the category "Houses" on the lower left, which does not include points for the Ascendant or MC.

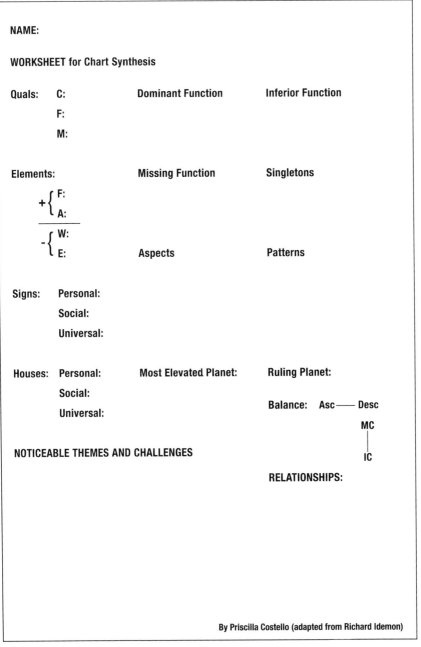

Figure 5. Sample Astrological Worksheet

Step Three: Integrate Left- and Right-Brain Perspectives

The final step is the actual synthesis. Repeated themes gain strength as you see similar messages conveyed by different factors in the horoscope. You also weigh these against potentials that suggest other themes. To determine and articulate all these factors, bounce back and forth between both sides of your brain as you put the pieces together, and use the encoded information as a springboard for (hopefully) inspired interpretation. If you get lost at any time, refocus on the worksheet or glance at the chart again. Other strategies include thinking about an image or metaphor expressing some part of the horoscope, or distracting your conscious mind by taking a break or researching a particular component of the horoscope in books or online.

Because every chart is unique, the same chart factor (planet, sign, house, aspect) rarely works in the same way for everyone. With so many possibilities embedded in any one, both experience and intuition can open your mental doors and enable you to make statements that resonate.

CHAPTER SIX

Example:
Oprah Winfrey's Horoscope

Step 1: What is striking about this chart at first glance? The planets are fairly well spread out, with a cluster in Aquarius in the second house, and two planets each in the tenth and eleventh houses. With seven of ten planets in three houses, issues around money and values, public career, and social and community involvements are especially important to her.

The Sun is conjunct Venus, the only conjunction in the chart. Aquarians can be cold and emotionally controlled, but the tie to Venus gives warmth and an emotionally outgoing personality—a paradox! At times she may be intellectually tough, insisting that people adopt certain ideas to better themselves, while at other times she may be compassionate and understanding. Her motivation for improving society may not be just intellectual altruism (Aquarius), but genuine loving concern (Venus). Doing charitable or volunteer work is likely to attract others' support and lead to heartfelt friendships.

The ascending sign is Sagittarius as well as the Moon, making Oprah a "double Sagittarius." The Ascendant is twenty-nine degrees; both the first and last degree of any sign give special intensity. Sagittarius has equal weight with the Aquarius bundle. This too lends warmth, as Sagittarius' confidence, enthusiasm, and optimism moderate the Aquarian chill and point to travel, education, or philosophical inquiry as specific avenues to transform herself and society.

Sagittarius rising radiates positive and magnanimous energy, with its ruler Jupiter lending generosity, confidence, and natural leadership. It is often found in charts of people whose drive to expand and encompass more leads to overdoing or excess, and, on a literal physical level, a struggle with physical weight. They are especially prone to "thunder thighs" (the Jupiter-ruled part of the body).

With those Aquarius planets plus two in Scorpio and one in Leo, Oprah has a lot of fixed energy; in fact, three of these planets form a T-square. While fixed energy lends determination, persistance, and management ability, the T-square implies that the factors are at odds with each other and can create problems in her life. The same

Oprah Winfrey

Natal Chart
Jan 29, 1954
4:30 am CST +6:00
Kosciusko, Mississippi
33°N03'127" 089°W35'15"
Geocentric
Tropical
Placidus
Mean Node

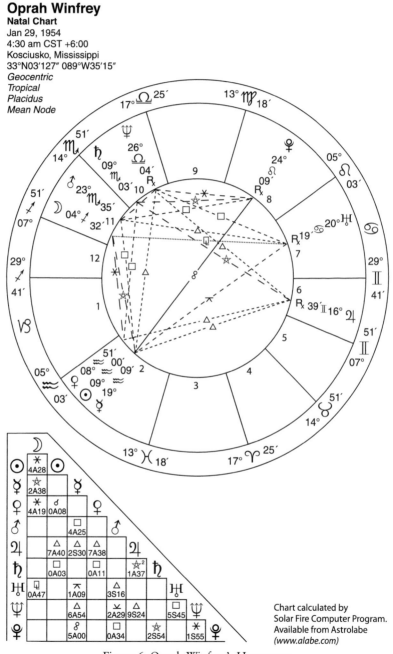

Chart calculated by
Solar Fire Computer Program.
Available from Astrolabe
(www.alabe.com)

Figure 6. Oprah Winfrey's Horoscope

NAME: *Oprah Winfrey*

WORKSHEET for Chart Synthesis

Quals:	**C:** 3	**Dominant Function**	**Inferior Function**
	F: (7)	*Fixed*	*Cardinal*
		Air	*Earth (Water)*
	M: 5	*Yang (+)*	*Personal Signs*
		Universal signs & houses	

Elements: **Missing Function**   **Singletons**

$(12)\ +\begin{cases} \text{F: } 4 \\ \text{A: } (8) \end{cases}$ *No Earth*   —

$3\ -\begin{cases} \text{W: } 3 \\ \text{E: } — \end{cases}$

Aspects   **Patterns:** *Grand* △

T square:

$1\ \vartheta - 1\ \mathcal{8}$

Signs: **Personal:** 3 $5\ \hbar - 1\ \square - no\ \angle = 6$

$6\ \triangle - 3\ \ast \quad = 9$

Social: 5 $1\ \pi - 1\ \angle$

Universal: (7) $2\ \star - 1\ bi\ \star$

Houses: **Personal:** 4   **Most Elevated Planet:**   **Ruling Planet:** ♃

Social: 4   Ψ

Universal: 5   **Balance:** $\text{Asc}\ \dfrac{(6)}{4}\ \text{Desc}$

$\begin{array}{c} \text{MC} \\ (7)\ \big|\ 3 \\ \text{IC} \end{array}$

NOTICEABLE THEMES AND CHALLENGES

emphasized 2nd house (+10, +11)   **RELATIONSHIPS:**

♄ *in 10th*   *29° ♊ on Desc.- ruler* ☿

Ψ$_{Rx}$ *in 10th*   *in ♒ in 2nd house*

♀ *in 8th*   ♅ *in 7th*

♅ *in 7th*

☉ *in ♒ in 2nd -* ♂ ♀, ♄ ♄

      ⚹ ☽, △ ♃

☽ *in ♐ in 11th -* ♇ ♅

      ⚹ ♀, ⚹ ☿

By Priscilla Costello (adapted from Richard Idemon)

Figure 7. Astrological Worksheet for Oprah Winfrey

planet at one end of the T-square (Mercury) also participates in a grand trine with Neptune and Jupiter, making Mercury the pivotal link, possibly providing solutions or relief from tension. All of these placements are in air, which seems the dominant element, so the dilemmas may be initially worked out mentally.

Note that I am making no final deductions about these observations, simply installing them in my memory banks, since initial speculations can be modified by more detailed analysis.

Step 2: Now draw on previous material in this book to assess the horoscope. To do this, start by calculating the balance of elements and qualities, and sign and house placements, and record the totals on the worksheet as shown on page 129. Later, select statements from lists in Part I for possible expressions of the planets' sign and house placements, and their aspects.

To remind yourself that the Sun, Moon, and Ascendant ruler all get an extra point, put a dot next to each of them. First, count points for qualities of the signs containing planets. On the worksheet for Oprah, C (for cardinal) will get three: one for Uranus in Cancer, one for Neptune in Libra, and one for the MC, also in Libra. Cancer and Libra are the only two cardinal signs represented. F (for fixed) gets the majority, seven: four for the Aquarius placements (remember to give two for the Sun), one for Pluto in Leo, and two for Saturn and Mars in Scorpio. M (for mutable) gets five: three for the Sagittarius planets (including two for the Moon), and two for Jupiter as the ruler of the ascending sign.

Seven points in fixed signs confirms our initial observation that Oprah has dominance in this quality. She definitely does have the capability to stabilize, manage, and sustain anything that she creates. The down side of so much fixed energy is tendencies to be stubborn, resist change, and be slow to adapt to new situations.

Under Elements, F (for fire) gets four points: two for the Moon in Sagittarius, one for the Ascendant in Sagittarius, and one for Pluto in Leo. A (for air) gets an unusually high number, eight: one for Venus, two for the Sun, and one for Mercury, all in Aquarius; two for Jupiter (as Ascendant ruler); and two for MC and Neptune in Libra. W (for water) gets three: one for Uranus in Cancer, and two for Mars and Saturn in Scorpio. E (for earth) has no points at all!

Positively, so much air intensifies her interest in ideas and talents for communicating and teaching. It potentially endows her with mental objectivity and clarity, social adeptness, and the ability to cooperate and coordinate activities with diverse people. Negatively, so much air can generate an overactive mind that worries and weighs options to the point of mental paralysis. It can be over-adaptive, glib and facile, and dissociated from the body due to "living in the head." With no earth in her horoscope to ground her, the latter is likely. When an element is missing, surrounding yourself with people who have abundance in that element familiarizes you with it, and encourages you to access and express its qualities yourself.

When you add the fire and air points together, you get a very high positive/yang result: twelve. Water and earth energy combined is a mere three. So Oprah is operating with a great deal of active, masculine, and extroverted energy, bestowing assertiveness, confidence, courage, and enterprise. Dominance in masculine, fixed, and air gives an "over-influence" of Aquarius, the only sign combining all these qualities, making Oprah a true Aquarian. She definitely fits the description of Aquarius given earlier, seeking "to transform the culture or community," making intellectual efforts "to improve society, driven by altruism that seeks not only tolerance but full social integration."

Under Signs, personal signs, the ones from Aries to Cancer, total three (two for Jupiter and one for Uranus); social signs, from Leo to Scorpio, are allotted five; and universal signs, from Sagittarius through Pisces, get the biggest number, seven. Oprah is very much oriented to the greater-than-personal world.

For Houses, personal houses (one through four) get four points; social houses (five through seven) also get four, and universal houses (nine through twelve) get five. These numbers are close, so nothing is outstanding here.

Now write down categories with very high or very low numbers under Dominant and Inferior Functions in the upper right of the worksheet. Dominant functions are those the person feels comfortable expressing because they seem easy or flow naturally. The inferior functions, with few or no energies, are psychologically dynamic because the person is pressured to balance these with the stronger ones. For Oprah, the dominant factors are fixed quality, air element, yang (or masculine) energy, and universal signs (and, to a slight degree, houses). She is weaker in cardinal energy (only two planets here), earth (and to a lesser degree, water), and personal signs.

Oprah has no singletons, but these are extraordinarily significant if they occur. A singleton is only one planet in any of the categories, which means it carries total responsibility for representing it.

Surprisingly, this magnifies rather than underplays the planetary energy. Sometimes it dominates the personality, being exaggerated in importance and urging you to satisfy its needs to the exclusion of others. If it is too compulsive and hard to gratify, you may initially repress it, though the issues will eventually surface with even greater force.

Oprah does have a Missing Function—no earth. Like singletons, missing functions can tilt a life in the direction of what is not there. The psychological drive to "fill in the empty space" is even more compelling than a singleton, leading either to overcompensation or going unconscious. Having singletons or missing functions may not be detrimental, as many creative geniuses have these in their horoscopes. For example, Einstein had a quadruple singleton Uranus. Both Errol Flynn and Richard Burton (the actor) had a singleton Mars, each playing heroic and sexually magnetic characters.

Missing earth sensitizes Oprah to the physical level where you satisfy your sensual desires, deal with money, and accomplish practical things in the material sphere. With no earth energy, Oprah may obsess about physical security, safety, and comfort, and be forced again and again to rethink her attitudes toward her body and its functions. With no earth, you have to remind yourself constantly of physical needs like eating well, exercising, and getting enough rest. As your life unfolds, you can become adept in these areas. Other famous people with no earth in their charts are Hugh Hefner (!), Mozart (famously bad at handling money), Jackie Gleason (who struggled with his weight), and Gloria Swanson (who carried suitcases full of vitamins with her when she traveled).

Under Aspects in the center of the worksheet, note the numbers of each type of aspect, looking for high or low totals, or absence of a particular aspect altogether. While Oprah has five squares, she also has six trines and three sextiles, suggesting that challenges are outweighed by talents and opportunities.

For Patterns, consider that T-square and the grand trine more closely. In the T-square, Mercury is in dignity in Aquarius and displays many positive qualities: mental brilliance and insight, creativity, open-mindedness, the capacity to think independently, and outstanding ability to synthesize and solve problems. It can also get lost in abstraction, be arrogantly sure of the superiority of its ideas, and think that any difficulty can be resolved by changing thoughts and attitudes.

In the T-square, Mercury is about ninety degrees from Mars. The earlier section on Aspects noted that this can coincide with a sharp, perceptive mind—one quick to reply and good in debate, all wonderful qualities for a talk-show host. But it can also be sharply critical, quick-tempered, and egotistically invested in its ideas, as well as endlessly talkative. The mind is so quick to leap to conclusions that it can be impatient with others who are slower to get the point.

Mercury also opposes Pluto, lending the mind intensity, an ability to sustain focus deeply or at length, and the mental power to influence or persuade in advertising, education, politics, or public relations. This is quite different from the aspect to Mars, which wants to make instant decisions and speak quickly, while Pluto wants to take time to consider before responding.

Mercury is the common link between the T-square and the grand trine, which pulls in Jupiter and Neptune. The Mercury-Neptune trine bestows intuitive thinking, an imaginative mind, and the ability to articulate inspiring dreams or visions in words. Mercury's easy aspect to Jupiter magnifies these potentials (it always expands what it touches), and also lends nobility, optimism, and broad-mindedness to thinking. The mind is naturally philosophical and loves learning.

Not only does the T-square contain a paradox within itself, but the grand trine also presents another contradictory set of probabilities. While Mercury-Mars can be impatient and assertive and Mercury-Pluto is determinedly sure of the rightness of ideas to be imposed on others, Mercury-Jupiter can be tolerant and rather laissez-faire, having a forgiving mental outlook and letting people believe what they wish. The aspect to Neptune could reinforce this, being potentially more attuned to the emotion behind the words and disinclined to speak.

However, if the Mercury-Jupiter manifests as self-righteousness, arrogance, and a sense of unquestioned authority, it may combine with the less attractive possibilities of Mercury in Aquarius, and the Mercury-Mars and Mercury-Pluto hard aspects. Oprah does not seem to have done this, although an aspect's more difficult potentials are often encountered early in life. Years ago, she may have encountered them in others or have moderated these tendencies in herself. In sum, all the Mercury aspects indicate that Oprah has outstanding talents for communication and powerful influence as an inspiring role model.

You can do the same type of analysis with the other planets in the chart, balancing their easy and hard aspects, paying special attention to personal planets connected to transpersonal energies. If you need more clarity or depth of interpretation at this point, do some research. One of the most insightful sources is chapter 6 of *Astrology, Karma, and Transformation: The Inner Dimensions of the Birth Chart* by Stephen Arroyo, which gives extensive details about personal planets (Sun through Mars) linked to Uranus, Neptune, and Pluto. When I first began to probe charts, I made detailed notes on aspects like these from many books in order to gain more depth in interpretation.

Step 3: Now put the chart back together, balancing your written notes or memorized information with your intuitive deductions about character and life events. In scientific language, dance back and forth between both sides of your brain; in astrological terms, engage your Virgo-Pisces polarity—or create a harmonious relationship between Mercury (Virgo's ruler) and Neptune (Pisces' ruler).

When reading your own chart, you may immediately recognize aspects of yourself embodied in the symbolism and also struggle to understand and accept what seems unfamiliar. You are bringing into consciousness what may still be unconscious. At first, you may over-focus on more difficult combinations, but keep reminding yourself of the positives. The chart is a diagram of your own inner psychic structure; engaging astrology is, in itself, a way of increasing your awareness of both strengths and weaknesses. Considering the range of possible expressions and matching them to life events and circumstances brings clarity about how far along you are in the process of transmuting challenges into strengths. It can be heartening to realize the progress you have made in certain areas.

When reading someone else's horoscope, be cautious for three reasons. First, you may not know that person's level of consciousness, and you can only do a limited reading for someone whose awareness is greater than your own. Second, the chart represents the individual's evolutionary stage at birth. In the intervening years, the person may have grown through psychotherapy, psychological self-analysis, intense bodywork, or simply deeply considering and absorbing life's lessons. Some of your interpretation may have been true for that person earlier in life, as a child, teen, or young adult, but may not be relevant now. Third, and most important, is that astrological patterns predispose physical and psychological expressions; they do not predetermine them.

For Oprah the pre-eminent vehicle for transformation is likely the mind, given Mercury's dignity, key position connecting the T-square and grand trine, and status as busiest planet in the chart, making the most aspects to others. This means that she may recommend that others rely primarily on the mind to alter their life circumstances. Mercury seems to have blessed Oprah abundantly with its gifts of eloquence and persuasiveness, and cleverness in business negotiations.

So if you were talking with Oprah about her horoscope, what approach would you use? To start by articulating ideas about the Sun is a good choice, since people often have some general knowledge of their Sun sign. I personally begin there and go on to add "layers" to the interpretation by exploring the Sun's house position and aspects.

In Oprah's case, this means noting the contradiction between the Sun in Aquarius and its conjunction with Venus, already explored, as well as offering interpretations of the sextile to the Moon, the trine to Jupiter, and the square to Saturn. With the latter two, you encounter another paradox: the easy aspect to Jupiter promises luck and opportunities naturally arising from "being in the right place at the right time" without having to work hard for them, along with career success and expansion especially related to learning or teaching (like sponsoring a book club!). Yet, she has to watch for being involved in too many projects at one time, and being self-indulgent or overspending.

With the square to Saturn, however, nothing comes easily. It insists that she labor for rewards and overcome a difficult childhood—or low self-esteem, or obstructive males—to gain respect due to career achievement and money earned. While Saturn may make her a late bloomer and a workaholic, it also restrains Jupiterian excesses. It may also help compensate for no earth, since Saturn is a grounding energy. Though earlier in life she may have bounced between periods of optimism and pessimism, later she may have developed a mature ability to consider options carefully and make astute choices about where to invest her time, energy, and money to great success. Only talking with her would reveal how she experiences these issues now.

Planetary emphasis in the second, eleventh, and tenth houses means you should comment on their corresponding life areas. Two planets in the eleventh reinforce the Aquarian "vibe" of this chart. The Moon there suggests not only strong friendships with women, but also that the public becomes her friend. The tenth house is especially mixed, containing both Saturn and Neptune. Saturn expects absolute honesty and integrity or your career can collapse and your public reputation suffer (Bill Clinton has this in his horoscope). Neptune draws Oprah into charitable work and lends her glamor and charisma. A tenth house Neptune can bestow an aura of numinous fascination, so you become the focus of public adoration and an icon of inspiration (like Princess Diana, who also had Neptune in the tenth).

When weighing possible interpretations, look for multiple indicators in different parts of the chart. For example, what light can Oprah's horoscope shed on her choice not to marry Stedman Graham? The collective focus of her Aquarian Sun values wider connections with friends and community and needs much freedom. Gemini on the Descendant also likes freedom of movement and expression and is reluctant to commit. Even more significant is Uranus in the seventh house, which intensifies the need for personal freedom and prefers an unconventional partnership. With this, there can be periodic separations from a mate, with exciting reconnections. Oprah needs opportunities to interact with bright people and large groups, possibly through technology (Uranus rules television). Uranus is also in hard aspect to the Moon, suggesting that a disrupted childhood may have established certain emotional patterns, and also that Oprah derives some emotional satisfaction from creative or humanitarian activities.

An advantage to speculating about well-known people's charts is that their lives are public and usually well-documented. Reading their biographies, both authorized and unauthorized, along with studying their horoscopes helps develop expertise in synthesis. But no story, biography, or astrological chart reveals the whole mystery of the appearance, being, and uniqueness of any individual. A geographic map is a flat two-dimensional representation of a grander three-dimensional reality, teeming with life and activity. Similarly, a horoscope both reveals and conceals the multi-dimensional, many-pieced puzzle of a human being. No matter how inspired or detailed an interpretation, there is no "last word" on anyone's chart.

CHAPTER SEVEN

CONCLUSION

THE SYMBOLIC LANGUAGE OF ASTROLOGY, with its cosmic reference points, speaks on many levels—spiritual, esoteric, psychological, and practical—with astonishing variety as well as specificity. Websites and books listed in the Bibliography can lead you in many directions: to deepen your understanding of the basics and add more factors to your analysis; to analyze one factor in more depth, like a dominant planet in your chart; or to gain insights into relationships, medical astrology, business and financial cycles, or historical correlatives to astrological patterns. If you are prepared and eager to engage the predictive dimension of astrology, look for works on transits, secondary progressions, or solar-arc directions.

Along with reading other sources, you can purchase your own software to study charts, or join credible organizations to receive newsletters and journals, or prepare for tests at various levels. In the U. S., the National Council for Geocosmic Research has a superbly developed four-level study program and administers examinations. They also publish excellent newsletters and themed journals, organize conferences, and have chapters in major American cities. For locations and contact persons, consult their website (*www.geocosmic.org*). For the truly ambitious, Kepler College in Seattle, Washington offers a four-year accredited B.A. degree in astrology and the liberal arts in a combination of online work and residential seminars (*www.kepler.edu*).

In Canada, the Canadian Association for Astrological Education sponsors workshops, teaches courses, and administers examinations (*www.thecaae.com*). In England, the Astrological Association of Great Britain is one of the oldest and most respected astrological organizations in the world. It conducts excellent conferences each September at a different British university, and puts out first-rate publications (*www.astrologicalassociation.com*).

These days, your options are many. You can learn independently through reading, or online by accessing websites run by recognized teachers, or in the stimulating company of others while taking courses together. A knowledgable and inspiring teacher, as in all traditions, can powerfully stimulate you, accelerate your learning, and save you time and money.

Final Words

You now have the fundamental components of the astrological alphabet that can enable you to analyze and synthesize horoscopes. Understanding your chart can encourage you to work with and through challenges, to develop your strengths and talents, and to grow gracefully into greater awareness of both your individual uniqueness and common humanity. Astrology bridges the psychological and the spiritual. Remarkably, every horoscope contains the same archetypal principles, so astrology supports the mystical truth of the unity of all things. Yet these universal elements are in a completely different arrangement in each chart, allowing for the wonderful spectrum of human diversity. Seeing that you are included as an integral and integrated part of the whole satisfies a longing for meaning and purpose as no other study can.

The benefits of pursuing astrology are many. Contemplating your own horoscope puts you in the position of observer—a powerful position that promotes a detachment that can enable greater spiritual progress. Comprehending your own particular pattern of strengths and weaknesses empowers rather than limits you. The more conscious you are, the more control you actually have in your life to make more informed choices. As in alchemy, you assist in the perfection or redemption of nature by transmuting your own energetic pattern into a more refined expression. In modern New Age language you "cocreate" your experience in harmony with the divine.

For centuries, many have intuited that there is a hidden knowledge, discovered by probing beneath the surface of things. This knowledge is encoded in symbols, like the inner gold of the alchemists or the prime numbers of the philosophical mathematicians. It is the DNA of the cosmos. As the preeminent language of symbols, astrology is the most elegantly developed system of correspondances revealing the creative design of the Universe and including us as the living expression of patterns of cosmic significance. The grandeur of the star-speckled heavens is mirrored in the inner beauty and light of the individual soul. Our bodies are made of stardust, and our souls forged in the heavens. Through studying the stars, heaven is truly brought down to Earth.

BIBLIOGRAPHY

Web Sites

For information about the author, author's lecture/workshop schedule, and other publications, see *www.priscillacostello.com* or *celestialsolutions.ca*.

Useful websites, some with substantial information about astrological basics, include:
www.alabe.com (for free horoscopes and purchasing Solar Fire Computer Program)
www.astro.com (see especially the articles by Liz Greene and Robert Hand)
www.mountainastrologer.com
www.stariq.com
www.evolvingdoor.ca (excellent articles on signs and retrograde planets, plus an astrology dictionary)

Books

For books, new or used, go to *www.amazon.com, www.abebooks.com,* or *www.astrologyetal.com* (a bookstore in Seattle, Washington). Here are some suggestions for further reading:

General Introduction and Interpretation:

Arroyo, Stephen, M.A. *Astrology, Karma, and Transformation: The Inner Dimensions of the Birth Chart*. Davis, CA: CRCS Publications, 1978.
———. *Astrology, Psychology, and The Four Elements*. Davis, CA: CRCS Publications, 1975.
———. *Chart Interpretation Handbook: Guidelines for Understanding the Essentials of the Birth Chart*. Ed. Jerilynn Marshall. Sebastopol, CA: CRCS Publications, 1989.
Campion, Nicholas. *The Ultimate Astrologer*. London: Rider, 2002.
Costello, Priscilla. "Ladder to Labyrinth: The Spiritual and Psychological Dimensions of Astrology." *Gnosis*, No. 38, Winter 1996. Reprinted in *The Inner West: An Introduction to the Hidden Wisdom of the West*. Ed. and intro. by Jay Kinney. New York, NY: Jeremy P. Tarcher/Penguin, 2004.
Forrest, Steven. *The Inner Sky: How to Make Wiser Choices for a More Fulfilling Life*. San Diego, CA: Astro Communication Services, 1989.
Hand, Robert. *Horoscope Symbols*. Rockport, MA: Para Research, 1981.
Idemon, Richard. *The Magic Thread: Astrological Chart Interpretation Using Depth Psychology*. Ed. Gina Ceaglio. York Beach, ME: Samuel Weiser, Inc., 1996.
Oken, Alan. *Alan Oken's Complete Astrology*. Lake Worth, FL: Ibis Press, 2006.

Planets:

Arroyo, Stephen. *Exploring Jupiter: The Astrological Key to Progress, Prosperity and Potential.* Ed. Barbara McEnerney. Sebastopol, CA: CRCS Publications, 1996.

Bell, Lynn, et al. *The Mars Quartet: Four Seminars on the Astrology of the Red Planet.* London, England: Center for Psychological Astrology Press, 2001.

Dreyer, Ronnie Gale. *Venus: the Evolution of the Goddess and Her Planet.* London: Aquarian/Harper-Collins, 1994.

Forrest, Steven. *The Book of Pluto.* San Diego, CA: ACS Publications, 1994.

Greene, Liz. *Apollo's Chariot: The Meaning of the Astrological Sun.* CPA Seminar Series. London: Center for Psychological Astrology Press, 2001.

———. *The Astrological Neptune and the Quest for Redemption.* York Beach, ME: Samuel Weiser, Inc., 1996.

———. *Saturn: A New Look at an Old Devil.* New York, NY: Samuel Weiser, Inc., 1976.

Greene, Liz and Howard Sasportas. *The Luminaries: The Psychology of the Sun and Moon in the Horoscope.* York Beach, ME: Samuel Weiser, Inc., 1992.

———. *The Inner Planets: Building Blocks of Personal Reality.* Seminars in Psychological Astrology, Vol. 4. York Beach, ME: Samuel Weiser, Inc., 1993.

Tierney, Bil. *Twelve Faces of Saturn: Your Guardian Angel Planet.* St. Paul, MN: Llewellyn Publications, 1997.

Houses

Sasportas, Howard. *The Twelve Houses: An Introduction to the Houses in Astrological Interpretation.* Wellingborough, Northamptonshire: The Aquarian Press, 1985.

Aspects

Tierney, Bil. *Dynamics of Aspect Analysis: New Perceptions in Astrology.* Reno, NV: CRCS Publications, 1983.

Tompkins, Sue. *Aspects in Astrology: A Guide to Understanding Planetary Relationships in the Horoscope.* Rochester, VT: Destiny Books, 2002.

Chart Interpretation

Alexander, Roy. *Chart Synthesis: Applied Interpretation in Natal Astrology.* Wellingborough, Northamptonshire: The Aquarian Press, 1984.

Marks, Tracy. *The Art of Chart Synthesis.* Arlington, MA: Sagittarius Rising, 1980.

Relationships:

Greene, Liz. *Relating: An Astrological Guide to Living with Others on a Small Planet.* London: Coventure Ltd., 1977.

Idemon, Richard. *Through the Looking Glass: A Search for the Self in the Mirror of Relationships.* Seminars in Psychological Astrology, Volume 5. Ed. Howard Sasportas. York Beach, ME: Samuel Weiser, Inc., 1992.

Sargent, Lois Haines. *How to Handle Your Human Relations.* Tempe, AZ: American Federation of Astrologers, 2006.

Political and Historical Cycles

Baigent, Michael, Nicholas Campion, and Charles Harvey. *Mundane Astrology: The Astrology of Nations, Groups and Organizations.* Wellingborough, Northamptonshire: The Aquarian Press, 1984.
Tarnas, Richard. *Cosmos and Psyche: Intimations of a New World View.* New York, NY: Viking, 2006.
Whitfield, Dr. Peter. *Astrology: A History.* New York, NY: Harry N. Abrams, Inc., 2001.

To Our Readers

Weiser Books, an imprint of Red Wheel/Weiser, publishes books across the entire spectrum of occult and esoteric subjects. Our mission is to publish quality books that will make a difference in people's lives without advocating any one particular path or field of study. We value the integrity, originality, and depth of knowledge of our authors.

Our readers are our most important resource, and we appreciate your input, suggestions, and ideas about what you would like to see published. Please feel free to contact us, to request our latest book catalog, or to be added to our mailing list.

Red Wheel/Weiser, LLC
500 Third Street, Suite 230
San Francisco, CA 94107
www.redwheelweiser.com

The Weiser Concise Guides

A series of books, edited by James and Nancy Wasserman, designed to provide clear and accurate introductions to the most important disciplines of the Western Esoteric Tradition. Each book is written by a knowledgeable expert in the field. Broad overviews are augmented by explicit instructions for beginning and enhancing one's practice. Each author discusses the relevance of the subject matter to the personal life of the reader. Bibliographies of the best work in each field are provided, allowing the reader to continue his or her studies with the most discerning authorities.

Alchemy
Brian Cotnoir

A guide to the theory and practice of alchemy with instructions on actually performing the alchemical work and setting up a laboratory for further experimentation. Illuminates both the spiritual and physical aspects of this ancient science and art.

Yoga for Magick
Nancy Wasserman

A guide to the theory and practice of yoga and meditation specifically designed for the practioner of Western disciplines such as Magick, Wicca, Paganism, and Qabalah. Includes extensive information on diet and suggestions for pursuing a healthy lifestyle.

Herbal Magick
Judith Hawkins-Tillirson

A guide to the theory and practice of herbalism, along with specific instruction in using herbs in magick. It provides a thorough overview of the relationship between herbalism, Qabalah, and astrology, along with a chapter on the magical system of Franz Bardon.

Check out:

www.redwheelweiser.com

or *www.studio31.com*

for future titles and more information on each book in this series.